HEAL THE SICK

Dr Barbara Leppard

Grosvenor House
Publishing Limited

This book is published by
Grosvenor House Publishing Ltd
Link House
140 The Broadway, Tolworth, Surrey, KT6 7HT.
www.grosvenorhousepublishing.co.uk

A CIP record for this book
is available from the British Library

ISBN 978-1-78623-345-5

For Jim

who has loved me and encouraged me for more than 50 years

and

in memory of Rev. Can. Paul Mtowe who died on August 8th 2018

a faithful servant of Christ and partner in the gospel

CHAPTER 1
IN THE BEGINNING

We proclaim to you what we have seen and heard, so that
you may have fellowship with us. And our fellowship is
with the Father and with His Son, Jesus Christ.
1 John 1:3 NIV

My story begins in the summer of 1981. I was working as a senior lecturer in dermatology at the University of Southampton with an honorary contract as a consultant dermatologist at the university hospitals. One Monday morning I went into the hospital to do a ward round with my two consultant colleagues as usual. One of the patients on the ward was a lady in her mid-sixties who had been admitted five months earlier with ulcers on her feet and legs associated with rheumatoid arthritis. Over the months the ulcers had got slowly worse in spite of our best efforts at helping her. On that particular day it felt like we had run out of options. I don't remember what we said to her, but we must have said something before moving on to the next patient.

At the end of the ward round I went back to see her on my own. I explained that we didn't really know what else to try to get her ulcers healed, but I said that I knew someone who could help her.

"Who is that?" she asked.

"Jesus" I said.

She replied, "Oh, He wouldn't help me."

I asked her why not and she said, "Because I'm not good enough."

I said, "You don't have to be '*good enough*' for Jesus to heal you."

1

I then told her the story from the Bible about the woman who had been bleeding for 12 years, who had spent all her money on doctors but had got worse rather than better. She came up behind Jesus in a crowd and touched his cloak, because she thought, "If I just touch his clothes, I will be healed."[1]

I said, "She wasn't good enough, but she knew that Jesus could heal her."

She told me that she believed that story from the Bible, but she didn't believe that Jesus would heal her. I said that I believed that He would and I asked her if she would mind if I prayed for her. She said she didn't mind, so I knelt down by her bed, placed my hand gently on one of her legs and asked Jesus to heal her.

Three days later, on the Thursday morning, when we did our next joint ward round, we took the bandages off her legs, and all the ulcers were healed! She was discharged home the same day.

Three and a half years later I met a friend of hers who asked me if I remembered her. I said that I did. She said, "Her legs are still alright you know!"

I have absolutely no idea why I went back to see that lady after the ward round or how I ended up praying for her. I had been a doctor for 14 years and a consultant for 4 years. I had never prayed with a patient before, nor did I know any doctors who prayed for their patients face to face. I had been a Christian for 16 years and although I believed the Bible to be true, I had always read it as if the stories in the Gospels were things that happened 2000 years ago. No one had ever told me that God was still doing those things today. I was completely amazed. I re-read the Bible from cover to cover, over and over again. In many ways it was like reading an exciting adventure story in which I myself was taking part. Seeing that lady healed totally changed my life and my expectation of what God was able to do.

---

[1] Mark 5:25-34 (NIV).

Over the course of the next year I prayed for a few other patients, simply asking Jesus to heal them. It was always with patients for whom straightforward medical treatment hadn't worked, or with a patient who asked me if I would pray. It wasn't very often, but on every occasion they were healed. I just thought that that was what Jesus did. It was what I read about in the Bible and it was what I was seeing before my very eyes.

A few months after praying for that first lady, I found myself telling the same Bible story[2] to another lady, this time in the outpatient clinic. The patient was a 34-year-old lady with nodular prurigo - a condition where you get itchy spots, which you pick. As you pick the spots they get more itchy. So you pick some more, leading to a vicious circle of itching and picking.

Her GP had written a letter asking me to see her. He said that she had seen a dermatologist somewhere else in the country 12 years earlier and that as a result of that consultation she understood that nothing could be done to help her. He ended his letter by saying, "I'd like you to see her though, just in case that isn't true."

I sent her an appointment and the first thing she said to me as she came into the room and sat down was, "I know there's nothing you can do for me. I didn't want to come and see you. I've only come to please my doctor!"

I asked her about her skin and she told me that she'd been to see another skin specialist and he'd told her that there was no treatment for her condition and that she would have to learn to live with it. She said that when he'd told her that, she'd felt unclean, and she'd felt condemned to being unclean for the rest of her life. It was at that point that I told her the story of the woman with the haemorrhage, who according to Jewish law would have been unclean the whole time that she was bleeding.[3] But I told her that the woman had reached out and touched Jesus' cloak and was healed.

---

[2] Mark 5:25-34 (NIV).
[3] Leviticus 12:2 (NIV).

She said to me, "Why did you tell me that story?"

I said, "I don't know. It just came into my mind."

Then she said, "Yesterday a friend of mine took me to a meeting at her church and a lady there was talking about that story!"

At the time my patient wasn't a Christian, but her friend had taken her to a church just the day before. So I said to her, "Well, you know, what you were told years ago, is true. As a doctor there is absolutely nothing that I can do for you. But would you like me to pray for you?"

"Yes please," she said.

I just held her hand and asked Jesus to come and clean her from the inside out and to make her well. I didn't give her another appointment. She hadn't wanted to come in the first place; I was certain she wouldn't want to come back. She got up to leave. She got to the door and opened it, but then she turned round and came back into the room and gave me a big hug. She said, "I didn't want to come and see you. I only came to please my doctor, but I'm really glad I came. Thank you."

Four months later I rang her up to see how she was. She said that when she left the clinic, for the first time in 12 years, she actually believed that she would get better. She said that during those four months (it had been summer) she had lost two stone in weight, she had bought herself a swimming costume and taken her children to the beach for the first time in their lives. I thought that sounded pretty good, so I asked her how her skin was. She said, "Well .... ! It's a lot better than it was." She must have sensed my disappointment at that answer because she went on to say, "Oh, don't be disappointed. I'm really glad God didn't heal me *just like that*' because during these months it has gradually been getting better and better and it has given me a chance to get to know Him. I have become a Christian and so has my husband; in fact my whole life is different! Thank you."

Lots of patients with extensive skin disease have told me over the years that they felt unclean. One 57-year old lady, who had had bad atopic eczema since she was a baby, said that she had felt unclean all her life - that somehow she wasn't fit to mix with ordinary people. Every six months, since she was a baby, she'd been admitted to hospital because her skin was so bad that she couldn't cope with it. While she was in hospital (on a general medical ward rather than a skin ward) she felt that she was treated like an outcast. For many years she had had to make her own dressings by tearing up bed sheets into 2-3 inch strips, applying a smelly paste to them and wrapping them round her body. Eight years before I met her she moved to Southampton and was referred to one of my colleagues.

I first met her when she was an inpatient on our ward. One afternoon I found myself sitting on the side of her bed talking to her about God. She told me that she believed in God but she didn't really know what He was like. I talked to her about Him loving her, just as she was. That He didn't see her as an outcast, but as someone He loved very much: someone He'd sent His only Son to die on a cross for. I told her the story of the leper who came to Jesus and said, *"Sir, if you want to, you can make me clean." Jesus stretched out His hand and touched him, and said, "I do want to. Be clean."*[4] I told her that Jesus was still like that and that if she would come to Him, He could make her better. She asked me if I would pray for her and I did.

Two and a half years later I met her at a meeting where she was teaching patients with eczema how to care for their skin. She told me, "Two and a half years ago a miracle happened. I came home from hospital and for no reason that I can honestly think of, my eczema didn't come back." She said, "It is so wonderful not to be scratching all the time, or to have to

---

[4] Matthew 8:2-3 (Good News Bible).

smother myself in greasy ointments. It's just a miracle. It can only be that God did something!"

Another lady who asked me to pray for her was a 32-year-old lady in a wheelchair. When she was 17 years old her mother had committed suicide. A few months later she tried to do the same by jumping out of a second-floor window. She didn't die but she broke her back and had been paralysed from the waist down ever since (hence the wheelchair). Because she had no feeling in her legs and feet she was forever injuring them. When I first met her she had been getting ulcers on her feet and lower legs for eight years. At one stage she spent six months in hospital trying to get them healed, but they didn't heal. Eventually I put her legs and feet into plaster of Paris so that they couldn't be injured. After 2-3 months her ulcers healed, but every time we left the plaster of Paris off they recurred. She hated having her legs in plaster because there was a horrible smell from the discharge from her ulcers. If I left her out of plaster new ulcers would appear. It was a catch 22 situation.

One day in the outpatient clinic when the ulcers were particularly bad she said to me, "Doctor would you pray for me? Would you ask God if He would heal my legs?"

Well, obviously I would. I put my hand gently on her leg and asked Jesus to heal her ulcers.

One month later she came back to the clinic and all the ulcers were healed! As she was leaving the clinic she said, "Aren't you going to pray for me today?"

I asked her what she would like me to pray for this time and she said, "Well, we ought at least to say thank you to God!"

So I prayed again.

Two years later I received a letter from her saying that she had not had any more ulcers and that she was so grateful to God for what He had done for her.

Patients were sometimes referred to the clinic by consultant colleagues from other departments. One Monday afternoon one of the surgeons popped his head round the door and asked me if I could see his mother in law who had terrible psoriasis. He had obviously assumed that I would say "Yes" as she was waiting outside the door! She hobbled into the clinic wearing a pair of bedroom slippers that had been cut open to allow her feet to fit because her legs and feet were very swollen. She lived in Oxford and was only in Southampton visiting her daughter. She told me that she had suffered from psoriasis for twenty-four years but one week earlier it had spread very dramatically and covered virtually the whole of her body. Her skin was so bad that the only option for treatment was to admit her to hospital. She was very reluctant to be admitted because she had travelled to Southampton to spend time with her daughter and her family. I asked her if she had any faith and she replied that she was a Christian. I said that I was too, and that I believed that Jesus was still doing all the things that He had done when He was here on earth. She said that she also believed that, so I suggested that we pray about her skin. She agreed, so I held her hand and asked Jesus to heal her skin.

Three weeks later I received a letter from her saying that the skin was virtually completely clear. She said it was quite unbelievable when only three weeks previously her legs were painfully swollen and uncomfortable. Her skin cleared completely and three years later, and again seventeen years later, she reported no further psoriasis.

I'm sure her son-in-law had expected me to treat her with conventional medicine, but he didn't say anything about her being sent home without any treatment. For the two weeks following the consultation I didn't see him once. It seemed odd at the time because we had offices only a few doors away from one another. I remember thinking, "He's avoiding me!" In all the years that followed he never once mentioned what had happened, although he continued to ask me to see his patients with various skin diseases!

During that first year of occasionally praying with patients, I met another Christian doctor at the hospital and we decided to meet together to pray once a week – on a Monday morning before the start of the working week. One morning I shared with him my concern for a 47-year old lady with pemphigus (a very nasty and potentially fatal blistering condition). She had been treated with very large doses of oral steroids and she had nearly died from their side effects (massive gastrointestinal bleeding, multiple infections and diabetes). The steroids had no effect on her blisters so anti-cancer drugs were tried instead (firstly azathioprine and then methotrexate), but again without effect. Although this lady was not my patient I shared that she was in a desperate state and that five months on we were no closer to getting her pemphigus under control than when she was admitted. We prayed for her three weeks in a row. On the third Monday morning I went from our prayer time to the ward to do my ward round. When I got to her bed she greeted me by opening her nightie and saying, "Do you believe in miracles doctor?" Her skin was completely free of blisters. I met her a year later in the local supermarket and she told me that she had been completely free of blisters and off all treatment for a year.

You may not think that these stories are anything out of the ordinary, but for me they were the beginning of an extraordinary adventure with God, which has continued ever since.

CHAPTER 2
ONE YEAR LATER

*So here's what I want you to do, God helping you: Take
your everyday, ordinary life - your sleeping, eating,
going-to-work, and walking-around life - and place it
before God as an offering. Embracing what God does
for you is the best thing you can do for Him.*

Romans 12:1 The Message

In 1981 I offered my ordinary, everyday life, including my work
life as a doctor, to God to do with as He chose. I continued to
do my work as usual, teaching medical students, doing research
and seeing patients in the outpatient clinic and on the ward.
Occasionally I felt that God was asking me to pray for a patient
and I did so. Every time that happened the patient was healed,
in a way which could not be explained medically. I just thought
that that was what God did. After that first year God began to
surprise me by doing different things. It was as if He loved my
patients too much to heal their skin diseases without dealing
with the underlying causes.

A lady in her 50s had been an inpatient twice, suffering
from both eczema and urticaria. It had begun when she was
on a world cruise with her husband. As soon as she returned
to England she went to see a dermatologist who gave her
pills for the urticaria and ointments for the eczema. They
didn't help and after eighteen months she was in such distress
with the itching that she was admitted to the ward for three
weeks. She improved slightly and went home. A few months
later she was readmitted and my colleague, who was looking
after her, asked me if I would see her to find out why she had
a problem.

I took her into the doctor's office and said to her that sometimes the kind of rash that she had could be due to worry or anxiety.

"Oh no," she said, "I haven't got any worries. I am happily married and we're not short of money. Oh no, there is nothing like that at all."

I didn't know what to say then, so I just waited in case she wanted to say anything else. After a bit she said, "Years ago I promised my mother-in-law that if she ever got old and couldn't look after herself, we (my husband and I) would take care of her. I told her that we would never put her into an old people's home." She said, "I told her, 'don't worry. If you're ever ill, we'll take care of you.'"

What had happened eighteen months earlier was that the old lady had become infirm and they had put her into a private rest home. Apparently it was a very nice place and the old lady was very happy there. All her friends had told her, "You've done the right thing." But she knew that she had broken her promise. And immediately they had got the old lady settled, she and her husband had gone off on a world cruise and she had developed her rash.

She told me that she had told that story to dozens of people and they had all told her, "You've done the right thing. That's what we would have done. It's much better for her; it's much better for you." But that wasn't the answer. The answer was that she needed to be forgiven for breaking her word.

I asked her if she had any faith. She said, "Yes, I'm a Christian." I asked her if she knew what the Bible says about forgiveness? Although she went to church regularly, she didn't know that she could be forgiven. I explained to her that Jesus had died on a cross in her place so that she could be forgiven, and she understood that. So she said, "Right, I'd better go and see my vicar then!" She immediately went back to the ward, got dressed, packed her bag and left. She went straight to the vicarage, confessed her sin to her vicar. He pronounced forgiveness over her and her rash disappeared straight away.

I saw her again ten days later, and her rash had not recurred. I spoke to her three years later and she had had no further rash. It is no wonder that ointments and pills had not worked because it wasn't her skin that was the real problem. The answer to the things that we've done wrong is to repent and receive God's forgiveness.

Another lady came to the skin clinic with genital warts. She came once a week and I painted them with podophyllin, which was the standard treatment at the time. This brown and very irritant liquid had to be painted very carefully onto the warts making sure that none of it got onto normal skin, which was why I was doing it personally. I had been doing this for twelve weeks when one day, while I was bent over her doing this, she said, "It's no good doctor, I can't go on like this any more!"

I finished the job, told her to get dressed and come next door into the consulting room. I didn't know what I was going to do next and sent up a quick prayer asking God for help. When she came into the room and sat down, I said to her, "What do you mean, you can't go on like this any more?"

She said, "Twenty five years ago I had an illegitimate child and I know I can never be forgiven for that!"

I got out my Bible and shared with her what God had done in sending His Son to die on a cross so that she could be forgiven. Obviously it was God's timing because she believed it and she went skipping out of the room. She stopped at the door, turned around to face me and said, "I didn't need to come and see you about my skin did I?" I had never seen a reaction like that before. Patients don't normally go skipping out of the room after seeing me, however pleased they are with the consultation.

I spent about an hour with that lady in the middle of a very busy clinic. Amazingly I finished the clinic on time and not a single patient complained about being kept waiting. It is so easy to think that there isn't time for digressions like that in the NHS. But if it is what God is doing, there is always time.

Jesus said He only did what he saw his Father doing,[5] and I was learning that that was what I had to be doing too.

A few months later I saw a 34-year-old lady from Guernsey. She had had psoriasis for seven years, but it had recently become very extensive. There was nothing I could do for her easily on an outpatient basis since she lived so far away, so I suggested that she be admitted for treatment. She couldn't come in to the ward straight away because she needed to make arrangements for her children, so I left it that she would ring the ward sister when she could come in. I asked her if she had any faith. She said, "No, but the children go to Sunday school!"

Six months later I found her in the ward. The first thing she said to me was, "Six weeks ago an evangelist came to our village and I've become a Christian and so has my husband!"

I thought, "Hello, God's in this somewhere!"

Her psoriasis was still dreadful, so I wrote her up for some treatment and left her in the good care of the nurses on the ward.

After a few days I saw her in the office and asked her why she thought she had psoriasis? She told me that at the age of seventeen she had an affair with a married man and had got pregnant. Her father insisted she have an abortion, but she didn't want to. The doctor at the local hospital told her that she could have the baby and that the baby could be adopted. She thought that that was the better option. But her father continued to encourage her to have an abortion, and eventually at twenty-four weeks she had a termination of pregnancy. She said it was really horrible. After the event she went back home and it was never spoken of again. Some years later she married and had a baby daughter, who she said was perfect. A few days after her daughter was born she developed psoriasis.

I told her that she needed to tell God that she was sorry for having an affair with a married man and for killing a child.

---

[5] John 5:19 (NIV).

I told her that she also needed to forgive her father for making her have the termination of pregnancy, and the doctors at the hospital for carrying it out. Obviously none of this would have been possible if she had been admitted six months earlier, but now that she was a Christian it was both possible and essential.

I asked her if she would like to pray with me about it, but she said she would go off and do it on her own. I also told her that she should give the aborted daughter a name and hand her over to Jesus. Well, she thought that was all a bit much. After all she had come into hospital to have her psoriasis treated not to have her past raked up.

Off she went back to the ward and we met again in the office a week later. She said, "Well, I've done what you said but I don't feel any different." But in that week she had decided that she did want to do something about the guilt that she felt, and now she was ready to tell God that she was sorry for what she had done. She told him she was sorry in front of me and I pronounced forgiveness over her. She then gave her little girl a name and in her imagination, handed her over to Jesus. And as she did so, she told me that she saw Jesus looking at her with kindness, and she knew that she was forgiven. Forgiving her father was much more difficult for her, but eventually she was able to do that too. Very quickly her psoriasis completely cleared and she was able to go home.

I never saw her again but two years later she rang me up to tell me her news. She said that after her first daughter was born, she and her husband had wanted another child but she had not been able to get pregnant. After five years they adopted a daughter and thought their family was complete. But she was ringing to tell me that she was now pregnant and was giving thanks to God for his kindness to her.

No one ever taught me to treat psoriasis like that! I felt so foolish. How could I have left God out of my work life for so long when He could do so much more than I could do as a doctor?

In Chapter 3 of "The Pilgrim's Progress," John Bunyan describes how "Christian" loses a huge burden from off his shoulders as he comes up to the cross of Christ. His burden rolls down the hill and disappears forever. When this happens "Christian" weeps for joy. He understands that his sins are forgiven, and he receives peace and the promise of eternal life.

Guilt is a terrible burden that people carry about with them, as I discovered by listening to my patients. Sometimes they had carried their burden for many years, and the burden had made them physically sick. Some of these patients were churchgoers but they still didn't know what to do with their guilt! The answer was to take it to the cross where Jesus died to pay the price for our sin. I have lost count of the number of patients over the years who have found this to be true, and like "Christian" in Bunyan's story, have shed tears of joy as the burden disappeared forever and their skin disease too.

CHAPTER 3
SABBATICAL

Ransomed, healed, restored, forgiven.

Ransomed, healed, restored, forgiven. That marvellous line from the hymn "Praise my soul the King of Heaven"[6] expresses the wholeness that only Jesus Christ can bring. As I began to pray for patients at the hospital I became more and more aware that there was more to the practice of dermatology than finding the right ointment to rub in or the right pill to take. I saw patients whose rashes disappeared when they repented and were assured of God's forgiveness; others with "hopeless" conditions for which I, as a doctor, could do nothing, completely healed after prayer.

In the summer of 1984 I had been working at the University of Southampton for seven years and wondered if it might be possible to take some sabbatical leave. I decided to go and see the Professor of Medicine, who was officially my boss, to ask about it. He said that it was usual to take a term off every seven years and that a holiday could be added to the term to have a six month break. He asked me if I had any ideas about how I would like to spend such a time. I explained that I had been seeing God heal patients in ways that I couldn't explain as a doctor and that I wanted to travel around the country meeting other people involved in the Christian healing ministry. I expected him to tell me that was not what sabbaticals were for, but to my surprise he encouraged me to do exactly that. He said that although most people used this

---

[6] Hymn written by Henry Francis Lyte in 1834 (based on Psalm 103).

kind of break to go to America to further their research interests, he had found over the years that doing almost anything different brought people back feeling refreshed and able to do their work better.

And so a new adventure began!

I had no idea how to set about finding other people involved in the Christian healing ministry in the UK but my vicar put me in touch with Reginald East, an Anglican priest who had founded the Barnabas Fellowship at Whatcombe House in Dorset. I had heard of Reg through reading his book on healing[7] but I didn't know him. I wrote to him explaining what had been happening in my life over the previous three years and he and his wife invited me to visit them. Over a meal they helped me plan my sabbatical. Reg wrote to friends all over the country, many of whom invited me to visit. One clergy couple in Manchester, who had a particular ministry of inner healing (also called healing of memories or healing of past hurts), invited me to stay with them for a month, and on two or three afternoons a week I was allowed to sit and watch them pray for people with deep emotional problems. Their ministry was very much based on the work of Frank Lake whose dynamic cycle of human relationships explained a great deal about why people had problems.[8]

Most of us feel the need to achieve something worthwhile with our lives – get a good job, own a nice house etc. If we do so, we come to believe that we are of value (someone significant). Our identity depends on what we have done (what we have achieved). Once we have achieved our goals we can provide for our needs and will be accepted by those around us. Of course if we don't achieve much, we are not acceptable and we come to believe that we are not of much value.

---

[7] Reginald East. *Heal the sick*, 1977, Hodder and Stoughton Ltd.
[8] Frank Lake. *Clinical Theology, a theological and psychiatric basis to clinical pastoral care*, 1966, Darton, Longman and Todd, London.

Frank Lake pointed out that this cycle of behaviour is completely the wrong way round, completely unbiblical. Jesus was fully accepted by His Father before he had achieved anything. At His baptism (before he had started his public ministry), as he was coming up out of the water, he saw heaven being torn open and the Spirit descending on him like a dove. And a voice came from heaven: *"You are my Son, whom I love; with you I am well pleased."*[9]

Frank Lake's dynamic cycle[10]

For us to be accepted there has to be someone to do the accepting and God's plan was for that to be our doting parents at the beginning - that they accept us as the most wonderful

---

[9] Mark 1:10-11 (NIV).
[10] Frank Lake. *Clinical Theology*, 1986, Darton, Longman and Todd.

and amazing human being. As well as being accepted we need someone to give us all we need (sustenance). Jesus said to his disciples that he had food to eat that they knew nothing about.[11] Jesus was accepted by His Heavenly Father and provided with all He needed. He was then able to fully enter into His significance (identity) and go and do what He was sent to earth to do (be crucified for the sins of the world). It should be the same for us. If we know we are accepted and that all our needs will be provided for, we understand that we are someone of value who can do whatever God has planned for us to do.[12]

I remember one young woman in Manchester who had had mental health problems for years. She wasn't able to work and felt that her life was useless. When she was being prayed for she remembered that her mother had tried to abort her on several occasions. She had grown up knowing that she had been unwanted and that her mother would have preferred her never to have been born. Using Frank Lake's dynamic cycle, it was obvious that she had never been accepted by her mother and felt of no value. But the truth was that even though her mother had rejected her (and still did so), God had not rejected her. He loved her unconditionally and said that she was fearfully and wonderfully made; that He himself had watched over her being formed in her mother's womb[13] and that He loved her.[14] For her to become well she needed to face up to the truth of what had happened to her, but to see that what God said about her was what was actually the truth. And indeed in time she was able to come to that point, forgive her mother and be healed of her mental illness.

Having spent a month seeing people healed of deep wounds from the past using Frank Lake's ideas I was later able to

---

[11] John 4:32 (NIV).
[12] Ephesians 2:10 (NIV).
[13] Psalm 139:13-14 (NIV).
[14] Isaiah 43:4 (NIV).

spend a week at the Clinical Theology Association annual conference to consolidate what I had learnt, and later still to complete the two-year Clinical Theology Course. At that stage though, it was still largely theoretical. I had learnt a good deal about inner healing, seen it work for individuals, and hoped that it would help me to help my patients when I went back to work.

One night while I was staying in Manchester I had a dream, which greatly disturbed me. I dreamt that I had been made the professor of dermatology at St John's Hospital for Diseases of the Skin in London. On my first day at work in my new position I went into my office and found that every available space was covered with pots. When I looked more closely I found that they were all full of dead plants and animals: it was horrible. The dream disturbed me not because of the dead plants and animals but because I thought that I had given up all selfish ambition when I surrendered my everyday ordinary life to God.[15] The next morning I shared my dream with Jean (the vicar's wife I was staying with). I explained to her that I had absolutely no ambition to be the professor at St John's and I couldn't understand the dream at all. As we talked about it I explained to her that I did want to be the best dermatologist in Wessex. She asked me why I wanted to be the best. Why did I need to be the best? I said I didn't know. She could have told me the answer to her question and the meaning of my dream, but very wisely she didn't. She simply told me to think about it.

A couple of months later I was at a four-day conference on Gestalt (wholeness) at Scargill House in North Yorkshire when I found out what the first part of the dream meant. During the second plenary session, after the teaching, we were asked to think of five things to thank God for about our mothers. I found myself unable to think of a single thing to

---

[15] Romans 12:1 (The Message); see Chapter 2.

thank God for with regard to either of my parents and I began to sob my heart out. The tea break followed during which I tried to "pull myself together." But it was to no avail. I found myself in pieces understanding that my parents had wanted a son not a daughter: that I had never been acceptable to either of them. I had, of course, known that all my life, but hadn't thought that it was a problem. I now realised that it had caused me to work hard in order to be acceptable, and that to be recognised as the best in the field – to be a professor – would have made me a significant person, someone of value. As people prayed for me in a small group, God sovereignly revealed to me that I was His child, totally pleasing to Him and able to achieve all He wanted me to do. It was years later, after I had, in fact, become a professor, that I realised what the rest of the dream was about. The dead plants and animals in the professor's office were to show me that following the ways and ambitions of the world lead to death, but that following Jesus leads to life.[16]

Until I had that experience personally I had assumed that I was OK. That it was other people who had problems and that I was there to help. I had only gone to the conference to see how I could help my patients better. But I learnt that all of us have issues from the past that need healing. During the rest of the conference I watched fascinated as other people there (including clergy, teachers, lawyers and doctors) were ministered to in many different ways. I also I learnt that just as the prophet Joel had prophesied,[17] God is able to restore to every one of us all the wasted years of guilt, anxiety, self-hatred, repressed resentments, rejection, inability to trust, inferiority, fear, failure and all the other things that result from not being loved unconditionally. It was another life-changing experience.

I was amazed then, and I am still amazed today at what God can do in people's lives if they will let Him. The natural

---

[16] John 10:10 (NIV).
[17] Joel 2:25 (NIV).

human response is to want to understand what is happening, but I have learnt over the years that God always knows what He is doing, and that we can trust Him to do what is best for each person who comes asking for help.

I was able to visit two Christian Healing Centres in the South of England, Crowhurst[18] and Burrswood.[19] I stayed at Crowhurst for a week on two separate occasions. The first time I went as a participant on a clergy-training week, which had a vacancy at just the right time. I lapped up the teaching and was invited back to teach on a similar course a month later. Twice a week at Crowhurst they have a service in the chapel with laying-on of hands for healing. On one occasion I was asked if I would assist by laying hands on those who came forward for prayer. I was told not to ask any questions – not to talk at all to those who came forward for prayer – because otherwise they might want to tell me their life history. I was told just to lay my hands gently on the person's head and ask God to come and meet their needs. I had never done this before in public. I felt completely out of my depth. How would I know what to say if I couldn't ask what the problem was? So my knees were literally knocking. I went up to the first person kneeling at the rail and said something – I've no idea what – and she began to cry. That made me feel even worse. I didn't know what to do. I thought I must have said something wrong. So I took my hands off her head and moved along to the next person kneeling at the rail. Quite soon the first lady got up and instead of going back to her seat, went out of the chapel by the back door. I saw her go. I felt bad about it but I didn't know what to do, so I didn't do anything. I didn't see the lady again that day, but I did see her the next day at tea. She was perfectly friendly but she didn't

---

[18] Crowhurst Christian Healing Centre, The Old Rectory, Crowhurst, Battle, East Sussex, TN33 9AD.

[19] Burrswood Health and Wellbeing, Groombridge, Tunbridge Wells, Kent, TN3 9PY.

say anything about the service the day before. The following Christmas I had a Christmas card from her with a letter inside. It said, "I got your name and address from the people at Crowhurst. I don't know if you remember me, but when you prayed for me, I started to cry. I'm sure you thought that was really strange, but I'd been suffering from Sjögren's syndrome[20] for many years and had to put artificial tears in my eyes every few hours. When you prayed I found myself crying." She said, "I couldn't stay in the chapel crying so I walked round the garden for an hour and a half crying my eyes out. Since then I have not needed to use any eye drops at all. Praise God for the wonder of His healing!"

Dorothy Kerin started Burrswood as a home of prayer and healing after she was miraculously healed of tuberculous meningitis at the age of 22. Her vision was to combine ordinary medicine and Christian healing so that patients would not just be made well physically but would become whole in body, mind and spirit. The Church of Christ the Healer at Burrswood is the only Anglican church in the country built and dedicated specifically for the ministry of healing. Services are held there every day and healing services twice a week. I went to stay there for 4 days. The day before I was due to go I ruptured my right soleus muscle (one of the calf muscles) playing tennis. I arrived on crutches and had to be moved from my allocated room upstairs to a ground floor room. My abiding memory of being there was of the kindness shown to me, and the huge teddy bear on the bed in my room. I'm not really a teddy bear person, but somehow its presence in my room symbolised the love and care of Jesus shown in that place, which is obviously one of their values.

The first disciples were obedient to Jesus' command to proclaim the Good News by preaching and healing.[21] They didn't

---

[20] Sjögren's syndrome is a disease where the patient can't make tears or saliva, causing them to have dry eyes and a dry mouth.
[21] Luke 9:1-2; 10:9; Matthew 28:19-20.

make a fuss about it. They just got on with it.[22] Until I went on sabbatical I didn't know any other doctors who were praying with patients, and in spite of being in various churches all my life, I had never heard a preacher say that we should expect God to heal today. In October 1984 I was able to go to the first John Wimber conference (Third Wave '84) at Westminster Central Hall in London - six days of amazing worship together with teaching and demonstrating how to pray for the sick and how to use spiritual gifts in doing so. For the first time in my life here was a man standing up in public proclaiming everything that I believed about God, and everything that I had seen Him do at work and more. And here he was saying that this is for everyone - that what I had seen God do at the hospital is the normal Christian life. It was another life-changing experience.

In between travelling around the country to meet people, stay with people and go on various courses I had plenty of time to read. I loved that. I devoured most of the books on healing available at the time. When I went back to work that was the thing that I missed more than anything else.

My six months off work came and went all too quickly. I did indeed go back to work refreshed and better able to do my work, but with a different perspective on what that work might involve, and how the church and medicine might work more effectively together. I wrote down a list of the main things that I had learnt and here they are:-

- God is wonderful. An amazing, loving Heavenly Father.
- Ephesians 1:17 says, "*I keep asking that the God of our Lord Jesus Christ, the glorious Father, may give you the Spirit of wisdom and revelation, so that you may know him better.*" It is only as I know God's

---

[22] Acts chapters 3, 5, 8, 9, 14, 20 and 28.

love and forgiveness myself that I will have anything to share with others. And I certainly did want to know Him better.

- The scriptural requirement for a good steward is faithfulness, not success. Faithfulness is success regardless of how it may appear in the eyes of the world. In other words, leave the outcome of my efforts to God.
- We are much more than bodies. That just as Jesus grew in wisdom and stature, and in favour with God and man,[23] we too need to be healthy in mind, body, and spirit, and in our relationships with others. That sickness in any of these areas can affect all the others, and that what I have to do as a doctor is to discover where the real problem lies.
- Matthew 9:5-6. *Jesus said, "Which is easier to say, 'Your sins are forgiven,' or to say, 'Get up and walk?' But so that you may know that the Son of Man has authority on earth to forgive sins, 'Get up, take your mat and go home.'"* We accept that God forgives sins: why is it so hard to believe for physical healing too?
- We are ineffective in the church because we have a limited theology about what God can do. Just as Jesus healed in many different ways – a word, a rebuke, a touch, forgiveness, deliverance – in the synagogue, in a home, in public, in private and from a distance – so He does today and there is no **right** way of doing it. In a TV interview in 1984, Bishop Morris Maddocks (advisor on healing to the archbishops of Canterbury and York), when asked what the Christian healing ministry was, replied, "It is Jesus Christ meeting individuals at their point of need."
- Medicine and the church need to work together if individuals are to know the wholeness that God intends.

---

[23] Luke 2:52 (NIV).

- In the church we make a big thing about witnessing as being the important thing, but what God says is important is that we should love one another. This is not just a good idea but a command,[24] and we need to be obedient. A doctor once said, "I have been practising medicine for thirty years and have prescribed many things. In the long run I have learnt that for most of what ails the human creature, the best medicine is love." "And what if it doesn't work?" he was asked. "Double the dose" he replied.[25]

- Jesus healed the sick because he loved them, not to produce a response (to make believers, followers, church members etc.). The only thing that was needed for the individual to receive healing was the simple, uncluttered belief that this man called Jesus could meet their need.[26]

- The widespread assumption is that anything that cannot be proved scientifically is either meaningless or not worthy of serious consideration, or at least suspect and well avoided.[27] The miracles of Jesus were not designed to make scientists gasp or to deny the laws of nature. They were signs of God's grace, signs of the impact of the Kingdom of God, signs of the compassion of Jesus.

---

[24] John 13:34; 15:12, 17; 1 John 4:11.
[25] Burrswood Herald, Summer 1984.
[26] Trevor Martin. *Kingdom Healing*, 1981, Marshalls, London, p. 43.
[27] David Watson. *Fear no evil*, 1984, Hodder and Stoughton, p. 75.

CHAPTER 4
FORGIVENESS

Our Father in heaven,
hallowed be Your name,
Your kingdom come,
Your will be done,
on earth as it is in heaven.
Give us today our daily bread.
And forgive us our debts,
as we also have forgiven our debtors.
And lead us not into temptation,
but deliver us from the evil one.
Matthew 6:9-13 NIV

When I went back to work I saw a schoolteacher in her 40s who had lost all her hair (alopecia totalis). You may not think losing your hair is a big deal, but when it is you, I can assure you it is. She was referred to me by one of my colleagues, who said he had nothing to offer her medically but wondered if I could help.

I said to her, "Have you ever thought about praying about your hair?"

She said, "Oh no! I couldn't pray for myself could I? I mean, it's OK to pray for other people but you're not allowed to pray for yourself are you?"

I said, "Where did you get that idea from?"

"Oh, I was brought up to believe that," she said.

I said to her, "The disciples asked Jesus to teach them how to pray, and what He said was, 'You start, Our Father.' We can come to God as our father and say, 'I've got a problem.' And later on in the prayer it says 'Give us today our daily bread.' Now that is not about loaves of bread coming in. It is an invitation, every day, to tell our heavenly Father what our needs are. And if Jesus taught his disciples to pray like that, He means us to pray like that." That was so far outside her comfort zone that she just couldn't accept it. Over the next six months I saw her several times, and gradually she came to believe that it might be true; that she could ask God to meet her needs. And about six months later she came and said that she'd been to the local church and spoken to the vicar and asked him if he would pray for her. He had done so; in fact he had laid hands on her head and prayed. This was a huge step forward for her. First of all in admitting that she had a need, and secondly in asking for help. Her hair in fact completely regrew. It may, of course, have regrown anyway. But it did. And she believes that God had a hand in that.

We so often recite the Lord's Prayer at home and in church without really thinking about what the words mean, like the lady described above. Asking for forgiveness seems to be quite straightforward once you understand that you can do so, and most of us are able to accept that we can be totally forgiven,[28] but somehow the next bit passes us by. If we accept God's forgiveness, He tells us that we have to forgive those who hurt us, which is not so easy. The parable that Jesus told about the unmerciful servant[29] makes it clear that if we do not forgive we will be in torment for the rest of our lives. And that really does happen.

I have seen so many patients whose lives have been ruined by not being able to forgive those who have hurt them. Patients tell me things like, "He doesn't deserve to be forgiven," or, "I can't forgive him. You don't know what he did to me." It's true, I may not know the full horror of what has been done to them, and from a purely human point of view the perpetrator doesn't deserve to be forgiven. But neither do we deserve to be

---

[28] Colossians 2:13-15; 1 Peter 3:18; 1 John 1:9.
[29] Matthew 18:21-35 (NIV).

2 7

forgiven. And yet God forgives us and it cost Him the life of His Son.

When we don't forgive those who have hurt us we may become full of bitterness and resentment over what has been done to us. These things spoil our lives and may cause disease. One lady in her 60s with a rare blistering condition told me that her husband had run off with his secretary twenty-five years earlier. Apparently he had lived a life of ease and she had been left very badly off. She was full of resentment at how he had spoilt her life. Another lady, with a self-induced skin disease, had married a Jamaican man and had gone with him to live in Jamaica. But she got very homesick and returned to the UK leaving her husband and three young daughters behind. She had always intended saving up enough money to send for her daughters to come and live with her, but she had never been able to save enough. Twenty-two years later she went back to Jamaica and was horrified to find that her daughters wanted nothing to do with her. She was now full of bitterness at her wasted life and was damaging her own skin. Both these ladies needed to forgive those who they saw as having spoilt their lives. My pills and ointments were never going to be the answer to their problems.

Some people deliberately choose to hang on to resentment and bitterness. But all the time that they do so, they are in torment and many of them become sick. I remember one man who had been ill for years. He lived in the same house as his brother but they had not spoken for twenty-five years. When I asked him what the original problem was he couldn't remember! When I asked him if it wasn't time that he and his brother sorted out whatever their differences were, he said he didn't want to do that.

Canon Jim Glennon from Sydney said that nothing contributes more to sickness than resentment, and more to healing than forgiveness.[30] When I first started praying for

---

[30] Jim Glennon. *How can I find healing?* 1984, Hodder and Stoughton, p. 54.

patients I knew nothing at all about the power of forgiveness in healing skin disease. As a doctor it had never before occurred to me that my patients might be sick because of things that had been done to them in the past, and even if I had known it, I would not have known what to do about it. Such a concept had not come up at medical school or in all my years as a doctor. I think I vaguely thought that since many of my patients had problems that I wasn't able to help them with very much, there must be something I was missing, but I did not know what it was. My sabbatical leave changed all that. I learnt that we all need to have our sins forgiven, but we also need to forgive those who have hurt us, whether unintentionally or deliberately. When we forgive we are not saying that what was done to us doesn't matter. We are not forgiving them to let them off the hook; we are forgiving them because God says we are to do so, and because it will hugely improve our lives.

A 42-year old lady with awful psoriasis for seventeen years came to the outpatient clinic. She told me that when she was two years old her mother was diagnosed with tuberculosis and had to go into hospital. Her father worked away from home and was unable to care for her so she was put into foster care. When she was ten years old she returned to live with her parents. By then her mother was a complete stranger and she found that she had a younger sister who her mother doted on. She could never understand why everything she did was wrong, and everything her younger sister did was right. When she grew up she couldn't wait to leave home. She married in her late teens and had a daughter of her own. It was six weeks after the birth of her daughter that her psoriasis began. I talked to her about forgiving her mother for abandoning her (even though it hadn't been her fault that she had been ill). I arranged to see her a month later. When she came back she said that it felt as though a huge weight had been taken off her shoulders. She told me that she found it really helpful to talk to someone about it, that she had started the process of forgiving her mother, and that it felt as if she had been cleaned from the inside out. As well as that her skin was amazingly better.

Another lady in her thirties had had atopic eczema since she was a few months old. As soon as she developed eczema her mother rejected her and spent all of her childhood telling her that she was dirty, that she wished she'd never been born, that she wished she'd had a dog instead of a child. I treated her for years without much benefit, glad to have helped her "cope" with her life of itching and disfigurement, but not able to get rid of it. I knew she was a Christian, but other than tell her to pray about her eczema I really wasn't a lot of help. After my sabbatical I was able to share with her what I had learnt. It was true that her mother had rejected her. That had to be faced, but it didn't mean that the things her mother said about her were true. What she needed to do was to forgive her mother for spoiling her life until now and then to believe the actual truth about herself, which is what God says about her.[31] Amazingly she was able to do both of those things and her eczema disappeared.

I loved my job, but after my sabbatical it was never the same again. Every day was a new adventure with God. One day I saw a 6-year-old boy with really awful atopic eczema. He had been seen by many doctors before me, both dermatologists and paediatricians, but his eczema did not improve. One of my surgical colleagues asked me if I would see him because the child's mother was a friend of his wife's. He said he wondered whether medicine and prayer together might help the child. When the parents brought him to see me in the skin clinic, they said they were both Christians. They said they believed that God can heal, but they didn't want to put Him to the test in case He wouldn't heal their son. I talked to them about what I had seen God do in bringing healing to many patients, but I didn't want to push them too hard in that

---

[31] Psalm 139:13-14; Isaiah 43:4; Zephaniah 3:17.

direction as they were not keen for me to pray for their son. So I prescribed bath oils and ointments for his eczema and suggested they went to speak to their vicar about praying for Mark.

One month later they came back to the clinic. All the ointments etc. that I had given them had made things worse rather than better. Mum and dad had gone to see their vicar. He told them he was ambivalent about whether or not God heals today, but said that he would pray for Mark and lay hands on him if that is what the parents wanted. But the main thing that came out of the meeting with the vicar was that Mark had never been baptised, and the vicar thought that that was the first priority! So when they came back to the clinic a month later they were pretty confused by the whole thing.

It was now the summer holidays, and during the school holidays there had been a mission to the village where they lived. Mark had gone to it but the parents had not. At the end of one of the sessions for children Mark had gone up for prayer for his eczema. Later, the parents had a letter from the church running the mission saying that Mark had been prayed for and if they wanted to talk about it further please phone them. Mum said they felt like they were being pressurised into something and they weren't sure they wanted to go there. So I tried to play the whole thing down and talk about other ways of helping Mark's skin. The consultation ended but for some reason they didn't go. Eventually I heard Mark whisper loudly in his mum's ear, "Couldn't we ask **her** to pray for me?" Mum then asked me to pray.

Jesus said, "*Unless you become like little children you will never enter the kingdom of heaven.*"[32] That little boy knew exactly what he wanted. I prayed for him there and then. The next time he came back to the clinic a month later his skin was fantastically better. His mother said that they had never seen

---

[32] Matthew 18:3 (NIV).

normal skin on his legs before, and his father said that he was now praying for him every night. From then on his skin just got better and better until he had no eczema left and was able to leave off all his medication.

I never went looking for patients to pray for at work, but all kinds of interesting situations occurred that I could not possibly have engineered.

One day I was sitting in the clinic and a man with psoriasis came in. He had been under different dermatologists and psychiatrists for years and had many problems. On that day he sat down and started to pour out his woes. As I looked at him, the thought came into my head, "What you need is Jesus." And I thought, "I don't know if I can tell him that."

And then he suddenly stopped talking and looked at me and said, "Was there something you wanted to say to me doctor?"

"Yes!"

Late one Friday afternoon I was going round the ward to check that all the patients were alright for the weekend when I came across an elderly lady sitting up in bed with tears streaming down her face. She was crying quietly, trying not to draw attention to herself. I asked her, "What is the matter?"

She said, "Nothing!"

So I sat on her bed and held her hand and asked if she would like to go somewhere a bit more private to talk. "Yes." So I took her into the doctor's office and she just poured out her problems. I just sat and listened. There were no human answers to what she was going through. And then she stopped and said, "Well, I've talked enough doctor. Now you talk to me!"

I said, "What would you like me to talk to you about?"

She said, "Tell me about the Lord Jesus!"

She wasn't my patient. I don't know how she knew I knew the Lord Jesus, but of course I did as she asked.

CHAPTER 5
KILIMANJARO CHRISTIAN MEDICAL CENTRE

*O Lord, our Lord, how majestic is your name in
all the earth! You have set your glory above the heavens.
From the lips of children and infants you have ordained
praise. When I consider your heavens, the work of your
fingers, the moon and the stars, which you have set in
place, what is man that you are mindful of him, the son
of man that you care for him?*
Psalm 8:1, 3-4 NIV

In the summer of 1992 I was asked if I would go to Tanzania for two years to teach in the about to be opened Regional Dermatology Training Centre (RDTC) based at the Kilimanjaro Christian Medical Centre (KCMC) in Moshi. The University of Southampton gave me two years "Special Leave" (unpaid leave) to go, so in November my husband Jim and I set off for Tanzania with the blessing of my work colleagues, our local church, and Bishop Morris Maddocks.[33]

We arrived in Moshi on a Saturday afternoon after a 22-hour journey. We were collected at the airport by Dr Henning Grossmann, a German dermatologist who was the head of the RDTC. He took us back to his house where his wife served tea in the garden. As we sat there in the sunshine, looking up at the snow-capped Mount Kilimanjaro and surrounded by beautiful flowers and many fruit trees, we felt completely at home. We were surprised to find that the tea was served from a vacuum

---

[33] Advisor on healing to the Archbishops of Canterbury and York.

flask. Later we realised that because the electricity supply was extremely erratic, everyone filled vacuum flasks with boiling water when they could. After tea we were taken to the local Lutheran Hostel where we were to stay for six days while our bungalow on the doctors' compound was being made ready for us. We went straight to bed and slept through the night until 5 am when the light came on in our room as the electricity returned. We had gone to bed in daylight and hadn't realised that there was no electricity, or that the light switch was switched on. On the Sunday morning we went to a local church with my new colleague, but the only words we understood in the service were "Alleluia" and "Yesu."

The next day, Monday morning, I started work. It wasn't at all what I had expected. The outpatient clinic was a single large room. Along one wall was a long table with a bench on either side. The patients sat on one side of the table and the doctors or students on the other (Figs. 1 & 2). There was a couch on the other side of the room on which the patient could lie down to be examined, together with a mobile screen which could be pulled around to give some degree of privacy. The only problem with that was that the screen cut out the light!

The dermatology beds were situated within the medical department on the first floor of the hospital. We had two rooms, one for men and one for women. The men's ward had ten beds, but on that day there were fourteen patients. Four of the men were on a foam mattress on the floor (Fig. 3). There were no curtains between the beds and no mosquito nets over the beds even though malaria was the commonest cause of admission to the hospital. There was no privacy of any

Fig. 1. KCMC. Outpatient clinic: dermatology student and patient sit opposite one another.

34

Fig. 2. KCMC. Outpatient clinic: several students working in close proximity.

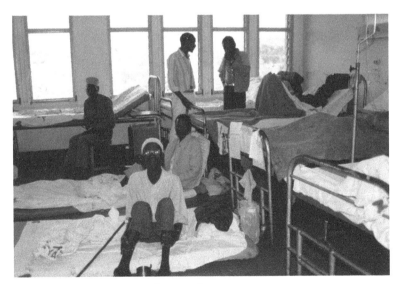

Fig. 3. KCMC. Men's dermatology ward.

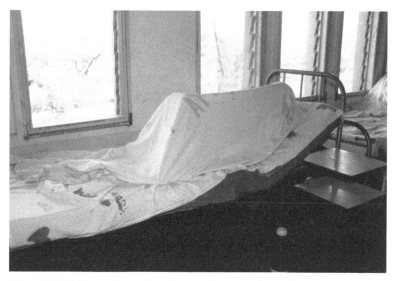

Fig. 4. KCMC. The only way to get some privacy on the ward.

kind for the patients and they would hide themselves under a sheet if they did not wish to be disturbed (Fig. 4). The women's ward was similar but with only six beds. At the end of my first ward round I wrote in my diary, "I can't believe that this is the best teaching hospital in the country!" After a week I decided that it was just not possible to practice proper medicine in these conditions. But I quickly found that that was not true. It was perfectly possible to practice good medicine; you just had to find creative ways of getting things done.

Health care in Tanzania is very different to that in the UK where we expect to be seen by a doctor when we are sick. In Tanzania there are 4 cadres of health care worker providing medical care:-

- Rural Medical Aide (RMA) – someone who has completed seven years of primary school education and then done a three-year medical training.
- Medical Assistant (MA) – someone who has completed four years of secondary education (GCSE level) and

then done a three-year medical training which is geared up to practising medicine within a rural setting.

- Assistant Medical Officer (AMO) – a Medical Assistant who has been working for at least three years in a health centre or district hospital and then done a further two years of medical study.
- Medical Officer (Dr) – someone who has completed six years of secondary education (A levels) and then done a medical degree at University.

Medical Assistants, Assistant Medical Officers and Medical Officers are all known by the title "Doctor," but work in different settings. In addition, traditional healers are found in every village and 80% of Tanzanians will go to a traditional healer before considering "scientific" medicine.[34]

Following independence in 1961, the president, Julius Nyerere, wanted primary health care to be the backbone of medical care for his country with help available to every family within walking distance (10 km) of their home. This is now provided by:-

- Dispensaries found in most villages. Here basic first aid, immunisations, obstetric care and treatment of common problems such as malaria and intestinal worms can be dealt with by RMAs.
- Health Centres, slightly larger than dispensaries, but also usually within a village, are run by MAs. The Medical Assistant will do everything that a GP does in the UK but will be paid very little. When we arrived in Tanzania the average wage for a Medical Assistant was £13/month.
- District, Regional and Mission Hospitals are small hospitals staffed by MAs, AMOs and doctors. There

---

[34] World Health Organization, *WHO Guidelines for the Evaluation of Herbal Medicines*. Manila, the Philippines WHO Regional Office, 1993.

are no specialists; all staff have to be able to deal with whatever comes in. These hospitals have laboratory facilities, X-rays and operating theatres, and provide all the medical care that most people will ever need, including surgery.

• Consultant Hospitals, staffed by doctors, many of whom are specialists, are large regional referral hospitals, expensive to run and situated in the four corners of the country. KCMC is one of these.

KCMC is well known throughout East Africa. As well as being a large 420-bed hospital, staffed by Tanzanian doctors and many missionary and volunteer specialists from around the world, it is famous for its educational role in health care. The RDTC was the tenth school at KCMC, the others being schools for:-

• AMOs
• Anaesthesia
• Health records
• Nursing and midwifery
• Occupational therapy
• Optometry
• Orthopaedic technology
• Paediatric nursing
• Physiotherapy

Most African countries do not have any dermatologists. My arrival in Tanzania meant that there were now five of us in the country (three in Moshi – Dr Henning Grossmann from Germany, Dr John Masenga from Tanzania and myself, and two in Dar-es-Salaam, both Tanzanians). Between us we looked after the skin problems of more than fifty million people! The Regional Dermatology Training Centre was started to combat this lack of dermatological help in Africa. It was the brainchild of Dr Darrell Wilkinson, a dermatologist from High Wycombe. He thought that it would be possible to train, not doctors, but Medical Assistants (or their equivalent) with enough dermatological knowledge to do the work of a dermatologist in all those African countries who had no dermatology services at all. And so a two-year residential course in dermatology, sexually transmitted diseases and leprosy was started. Training up Medical Assistants would mean that when they completed their training they would go back to the villages where they came from, work there as "Dermatology Officers" and train others in the local community. This would be affordable as MAs were not paid very much and they would be unlikely to leave their rural communities for the big cities to do private practice as they would not have a transferrable "medical degree." The International Foundation for Dermatology was formed and raised the money to start the project, which would eventually have a student hostel, a purpose-built dermatology building and even staff housing. But all that was in the future.

Student timetable for the first group of students.

	Group 1 (7 students)	Group 2 (7 students)
8-8.30 am	X-ray meeting where all medical X-rays from the past 24 hours were reviewed.	X-ray meeting. 2 students to prepare for the ward round.
8.30-9.30 am	Lecture.	Lecture.
9.30 am-1 pm	Skin clinic or practical procedures.	Ward round or bedside teaching.
1-2 pm	Lunch.	Lunch.
2-3.30 pm	Lecture/tutorial/ focus session or pathology.	Lecture/tutorial/ focus session or pathology.

When I arrived, the first fourteen students had been there for three weeks. They had been attending ward rounds and outpatient clinics but had had no formal teaching as such. There was nowhere for them to live; they were farmed out to other student hostels. There was nowhere to teach them; we borrowed a room in the School of Nursing for lectures and we used a side room on the ward for seminars. It was all a bit 'make do and mend' for someone used to teaching in an English University, but I very quickly adapted and organised a programme so that everyone knew what they were doing.

On Wednesday mornings from 8-9 am there was a "Grand Round" in the hospital's main lecture theatre, when there was a three-line whip for all hospital staff and students to attend. The various departments took it in turns to run these sessions and in addition any short-term visiting specialists were usually asked to speak. The very first week I was there I sat at breakfast in the Lutheran Hostel with Dr Kelly, a visiting gynaecologist from Birmingham. He was at KCMC to teach the local gynaecologists how to repair vesico-vaginal fistulae.[35] On the Wednesday morning I heard him give a fascinating account of how common these fistulae are after prolonged obstructed labour all over Africa. The young women affected are constantly wet and smelly as urine leaks through the vagina continually. They are often abandoned by their husbands and families and take to their beds to hide themselves away. Because they lie in bed with their knees bent they often get contractures and are then unable to walk. He said that he had been going to Ethiopia for two months every year for more than twenty years to operate on these women. When he is there he starts work every morning at 4.30 am, and because the staff know how much good the operation can do, they are very willing to assist him at whatever hour he wants to work. Indeed some of the staff, although not doctors, have been trained to do the operation when he is not around! Every week there was something interesting to learn at these sessions.

---

[35] An abnormal connection between the bladder and the vagina.

It cost about £7000 to train each student on the two-year dermatology course leading to an Advanced Diploma in Dermatovenereology awarded by the University of Dar-es-Salaam. This is very little money by western standards, but it had to be found from somewhere. The Medical Assistants who would become our students were on a very low salary and would never have been able to save such a sum of money. Initially the Commonwealth Office provided two scholarships for students from each of the commonwealth countries of East, Central and Southern Africa. Later, most scholarships were funded by dermatologists from around the world. The first group of dermatology students came from six African countries:-

- 5 from Tanzania (including 1 from Zanzibar)
- 2 from Kenya
- 1 from Uganda
- 2 from Malawi
- 2 from Zambia
- 2 from Namibia

There were 13 men and 1 woman in the group (later groups had equal numbers of men and women); all were Medical Assistants in their thirties apart from two nurses from Namibia. It was a huge sacrifice for them to leave their homes and families for two years, with just a two-month home visit, to do a research project, between the two years of study. They were all really keen to learn and worked very hard. They all helped each other out with whatever tasks they were doing and it was a joy to teach them.

Before I arrived I wondered if I would recognise any of the skin conditions that I would see. But I need not have worried. It was not that different to practising in England, except that HIV had to be considered in every patient and there were a lot more infections and infestations, and a lot less eczema, psoriasis and acne than I was used to seeing. That meant that treatment and prevention were a lot easier than in the UK, especially since old-fashioned remedies such as Gentian Violet and potassium permanganate were readily available and cheap. Topical steroids were not available in the hospital or in outside pharmacies. Vaseline was available if the patient could afford to buy it. Dr John White, one of my consultant colleagues in Southampton, kindly sent out two 50 kg drums of Vaseline and little by little we were able to get the basic ingredients with which to make up the treatments that were needed. When I had been there for three months two American dermatologists visited and brought with them 2 kg of hydrocortisone powder. We mixed it with John White's Vaseline at a concentration of 0.5% and within a week we had emptied the ward of patients with awful eczema. It was wonderful.

Before I started I wondered how I was going to be able to lecture on skin diseases without being able to show the students pictures of what the diseases looked like. But again it wasn't a problem. In the lecture at the beginning of the day I would teach them about, say, childhood eczema and then we would go to the clinic and see fifty children with eczema. Far better than just looking at slides! By 8 am on clinic days there would be up to 120 patients waiting to be seen in the outpatient clinic. And they would sit there all day without complaining until their turn came. We worked all day until all the patients had been seen. By 4.30 pm patients would often say to me, "Thank you so much for seeing me doctor. I know you've been here since early this morning. You must be tired!"

After we had been in Moshi a week we went to supper with my German colleague. As he drove us to his house we had a magnificent view of Mount Kilimanjaro, and when he drove us back home later the sky was clear and full of stars – a magnificent sight. I wrote in my diary that night, "I must re-read Psalm 8 before I go to bed. Although there are a lot of obvious difficulties, it is hard not to give thanks in all things, especially when the patients can be so thankful with so little."

CHAPTER 6
OUR NEW HOME

*Give thanks in all circumstances, for this is
God's will for you in Christ Jesus.*
1 Thessalonians 5:18 NIV

Moshi is a town, about the same size as Southampton, in Northern Tanzania just at the base of Mount Kilimanjaro. Six days after we arrived we moved from the Lutheran hostel to a very nice two-bedroomed bungalow (Fig. 5) on the doctors' compound, a short walk across the fields from the hospital. It was very sparsely furnished and without the basic necessities. Everything removable had been removed so the day we moved in we had to go into town and buy cleaning materials and other things that we would need, e.g. brooms, mops, buckets,

Fig. 5. Our bungalow on the KCMC doctors' compound.

bowls, light bulbs, a washing line, kerosene lamps, a kerosene cooker, a vacuum flask, Vim, bleach, insect killer, plates, cups, cutlery, cooking pots, sheets and blankets and some food. We had changed 200 US dollars into Tanzanian shillings in the local Bureau de Change in order to buy what we needed, but the bill for our shopping came to more than that. While we were trying to decide what to leave behind in the shop, the shopkeeper told us not to worry, to take everything and bring the money we owed on the following Monday when the Bureau de Change would be open again. We had only been in the country six days, but because we were English we were assumed to be entirely trustworthy!

When we moved into our new home we found that everywhere was crawling with cockroaches. We spent the first afternoon spraying them and stamping on them. I took all the kitchen drawers out into the garden and brushed them out thoroughly because they were full of cockroach droppings. I cleaned every cupboard and drawer with disinfectant and swept the kitchen floor on my hands and knees, as we couldn't connect the broom head to its handle without a hammer and nails. Before we went to bed we sprayed everywhere with "Doom" cockroach and other insect killer. When we got up the next morning there were dead or dying cockroaches everywhere, even in the kitchen cupboards that I had so carefully cleaned the day before. We worked hard all that day cleaning everywhere again before we were able to unpack our suitcases. Fortunately, someone on the doctors' compound soon found us a young woman, Dativa, who was willing to come in each morning and clean for us and generally look after us for the princely sum of £16/month. Later we employed a gardener as well at the same salary.

The bungalow was surrounded by a large garden with mango, grapefruit, guava, pawpaw, avocado and banana trees in the back. We tried to grow our own vegetables and the first year we were there we were quite successful, but after that our gardener, Simon, only wanted to grow maize and beans, which is the staple Tanzanian diet. We didn't really like maize meal (ugali), so most days we ate rice and beans, occasionally rice and lentils. Each day we collected fresh milk from the family living next door who kept a cow. The milk had to be boiled before we could use it but it seemed like a luxury to have fresh milk.

We arrived with just a suitcase each so the bungalow was pretty bare to begin with in spite of our shopping expedition. Six days after we moved in burglars came during the night. They cut a hole in the fence at the bottom of the garden, which separated us from the road, and then cut through the mosquito netting on the sitting room window to get in. There was nothing to steal and they left empty handed, but it left us feeling vulnerable and unsafe. When we reported what had happened to the hospital authorities they decided to put metal bars up at the windows, as there had been a number of burglaries on the doctors' compound. All that took time to arrange; meanwhile we had to light mosquito coils every evening to deter the mosquitos since we no longer had mosquito netting at the windows.

I have already mentioned the erratic electricity supply. Most days it was off for twelve hours or more, sometimes it was off for three or four days at a time. It wasn't until we had been there for three months that someone told us that there was a rota so that you could find out when there was likely to be electricity. Until then there hadn't seemed to us to be any pattern to when the electricity was on or off. Three evenings a week we went for Swahili lessons, which meant that it was always dark when we got home. That meant that if the electricity was off I had to cook on a single-burner kerosene stove - not easy when all the meat available was tough and had to be cooked in a pressure cooker. We mainly lived on bread and jam in the evenings for the first three months! And what to do in the evenings? We had no television or radio. The telephone simply connected us to the hospital so that they could get hold of us at any time of the day or night, so we couldn't phone anyone. We didn't know anyone to visit and we had read the four paperback books that we had brought with us in the first week. Of course I had lectures to prepare, but even that was difficult by kerosene lamp, as was marking exam papers.

It all took time to adjust. To begin with we didn't know anybody and colleagues and neighbours were slow to tell us what was available, where to get what we needed and how to do things. It wasn't deliberate; it was just that after a while people forgot how difficult life was when they had first arrived. One of our neighbours, an American ophthalmologist's wife, turned up one Saturday morning with a chicken (what a treat) which she had got from some nuns who lived and worked half way up Mount Kilimanjaro. Apparently they brought chickens and vegetables to sell every Wednesday morning at the International School (just around the corner from the doctors' compound). Until then we hadn't discovered the International School, but it was in fact a wonderful resource. It had a library from which we could borrow as many books as we wanted, a swimming pool and all kinds of entertainment – concerts and plays put on by students, staff and parents.

What people mainly did in the evenings was to spend time with friends. You couldn't phone to see if it was convenient to visit so you just visited. The Swahili word "Karibu" means "Welcome." In fact anyone who visited was welcomed with "Karibu" even if you were busy. One evening we went to visit a family and found their three teenage sons sitting at the dining room table doing their homework in a room as bright as day even though there was no electricity. In the middle of the table was a Chinese pressure lamp. We found out that they could be bought in the market for about £4, so we very quickly bought one for ourselves. It didn't solve the cooking problem but it transformed our evenings when the electricity was off.

Dr Grossmann had advised us to ship out our old Land Rover from England so that we would be able to get about;

what we hadn't envisaged was that it would take five months to arrive. That meant we had no transport, which was a problem since Moshi town, where the shops and the market were, was 5 km away from the hospital. But people were kind to us. A German doctor who lived nearby was going back to Germany for a month only three weeks after we arrived and lent us his Mitsubishi Pajero for the four weeks that he was away.

The Bible says, "Be thankful in all circumstances."[36] We should have been thankful. I had a fascinating job, we lived in a comfortable bungalow, we had help in the house, the weather was warm and sunny every day, Mount Kilimanjaro was a beautiful sight, but we were lonely and sometimes found it hard to be thankful.

After two months of seemingly non-stop work someone suggested that we might like to go to Arusha National Park for the day. It was a small game park only about thirty-five miles away, which included Mount Meru (4566 metres high). I asked Henning if we could borrow the RDTC Land Rover for the day. Initially he was extremely reluctant, saying that it was only for department business, but eventually conceded that it was essential to get away from KCMC now and again just for sanity's sake. What we didn't realise when we borrowed it, was that when Henning had last had burglars at his house they had stolen the jack and the wheel nut spanner for the Land Rover, so we had no tools in case of a puncture. We were new to Tanzania. We didn't know that you NEVER leave home without a jack and wheel nut spanner.

We got to the park shortly after 8 am and for the first two hours enjoyed driving around looking at the animals and birds. We didn't see any other cars at all and thought how wonderful it was to have the park to ourselves. Then we stopped the car at one of the observation posts by one of the lakes and got out to

---

[36] 1 Thessalonians 5:18 (NIV).

Fig. 6. Flamingos on lake at Arusha Park.

get a better look at the water birds (Fig. 6). When we got back to the Land Rover we found that one of the back tyres had a puncture. It was completely flat. What to do? We looked at the map of the park and decided that the nearest park gate was about two miles away. We thought that if one of us stayed with the car, the other could walk to the gate where we could, hopefully, telephone for help (no mobile phones in those days). In retrospect this was not a very sensible idea in a game park, although at that point we hadn't seen any lions, leopards, buffalo or elephants. We decided to have a cup of tea (from our flask) and pray while we thought about whether there were any other options open to us. Just when we had decided that there were no other options, a Volkswagen Campervan drove by! We flagged it down. It turned out to be a safari company van with a single lady passenger inside. She turned out to be a GP from Barnstable in Devon, who knew a good friend of ours who was also a GP in north Devon! We explained our predicament and she urged her driver to help us. He offered to drive Jim to the nearest garage to get help. I locked myself in the Land Rover and prepared myself for a long wait. Within twenty minutes they were back with a mechanic. He changed the wheel and we then drove him back to the garage to get the puncture repaired. Taking no thought to the fact that we could quite easily get another puncture, and that if we did so, we would be in the same predicament again, we then went back to the park and enjoyed the rest of the day there. Interestingly, we did not see any other cars for the rest of the day. Only one other car all day! What an adventure. It was a foretaste of things to come. We never ever went out on a trip without having some kind of problem; that was just life in Tanzania. But we never went out without a jack and a wheel nut spanner again.

CHAPTER 7
CHURCH

They went out and preached that people should
repent. They drove out many demons and anointed
many sick people with oil and healed them.
Jesus told his disciples, "As you go, preach this
message: 'The kingdom of heaven is near.' Heal the sick,
raise the dead, cleanse those who have leprosy, drive
out demons. Freely you have received, freely give."
Matthew 10: 7-8 NIV

What to do about church? After our experience on our first
full day in Tanzania, it was obvious that we wouldn't be able
to worship in an African church until we could speak Swahili.
So on our second Sunday we headed off to St Margaret's
Church (Fig. 7), which had a service in Swahili at 8.30 am and
a service in English at 11 am. The latter catered for all the
foreigners living in, or visiting, Moshi who couldn't speak
Swahili or who chose to worship in English. These foreigners
were from America, Europe, and the Far East, and many were
missionaries – doctors, teachers, road builders, agriculturists,
pastors and MAF[37] pilots, as well as students from many
African countries. In many ways it wasn't ideal at the beginning. There was an elderly Tanzanian pastor for the English
congregation who spoke very slowly and preached long boring
sermons; but after 6 months he was made a bishop and moved
away. In spite of the difficulties St Margaret's was somewhere
we could belong and begin to make friends. Once a month

---

[37] Missionary Aviation Fellowship.

Fig. 7. St. Margaret's Church, Moshi.

there was a "pot luck" lunch in someone's garden after the service and that turned out to be a good place to get to know people.

In April 1993 the church had its Annual General Meeting and Jim was put on the PCC[38] and also on the combined church council for the English and Swahili congregations. I was asked to arrange the food for a leaving party for a teacher who was going back to England! No one asked us what we were good at; it was just assumed that Jim would be good at churchy things and I would be good at cooking, neither of which were actually true. At the end of the meeting the pastor asked if there was anyone in the congregation who knew anything about the Holy Spirit who could speak at the combined Swahili/English service on the Day of Pentecost. I volunteered, and to my surprise my offer was accepted.

There had been no sermons in the previous six months like the one I was about to give and I was a bit anxious about how

---

[38] Parochial Church Council.

it would be received. I asked God to show me in the night if I had heard him correctly, and that night I had a dream. In the dream I came home from work, and as I opened the front door a big female lion leapt out. I rushed indoors, locked the door, and leant against it panting with relief. Then I heard an enormous roar. When I looked up there was a huge male lion in the corner of the sitting room. I rushed through the room and out the other side and locked that door too. The lion went on roaring and I was terrified. I didn't know what to do. Then the lion spoke to me and asked me to go back in the room and unlock the door so that he could go out. I didn't want to do that because I was afraid. I tried to devise all kinds of ways of opening the door without going back into the room. For example, I climbed up into the roof space, made a hole in the ceiling above the front door and let down a key on a piece of stiff wire, but try as I might, I couldn't get the key to turn in the lock. It just wasn't possible. In the end I gave in, and although I was absolutely terrified, I went back into the room and opened the front door, and the lion walked out. I then woke up and it was pouring with rain.

What did the dream mean? I thought God was saying, "Do you want to be safe or will you be obedient?" Actually, that was a good summary of what I had been going to say in my sermon the next day, so I took that as confirmation from God that what I'd prepared was correct. The rain I think was a symbol of the Holy Spirit's abundance that would come if I was willing to be obedient.

I had planned the service with the pastor of the Swahili congregation but the service was actually led by our pastor. He took no notice of what had been planned and plodded slowly through the normal "Morning Prayer" service first in English and then in Swahili the way he always did at combined services. I had a very nice man from the Co-operative College translating for me for the sermon, and it was fun speaking in tandem. I'm not sure how it went down. At the end I gave an opportunity for those who wanted to repent of wanting a safe life or those who wanted more of the Holy Spirit to stand and be prayed for. Only five people responded. The rest just looked at me expressionless. Two or three people walked out in the middle. I don't know why. Neither pastor said anything about the sermon afterwards, so obviously it wasn't what they were expecting. The congregation was obviously not used to participating in any way. When I asked them to be quiet for a minute or two to think about what I'd said, the two pastors sitting behind me immediately knelt down to pray. I didn't quite know what to make of it all, but I think I did what God was saying to do. The only encouraging thing was that afterwards a Tanzanian pastor who turned out to be the Rural Dean, and who had been visiting that morning, came up to me and said that for the last week he had been dreaming of having a healing ministry in the church and that God had told him that a mzungu[39] would head it up. And he thought I might be that mzungu! He told me to think about it.

Three of the five people who responded to my sermon were students from KCMC. A month later I asked them what had happened to them since Pentecost. One said that she had noticed a new willingness to obey God; one said that she woke up in the mornings longing to read her Bible and pray; the third said he had found a new companionship with Jesus.

After our pastor was made a bishop, various members of the congregation took the services and preached. Sermons were really good from then on and there was tremendous variety in the services as people used their many gifts. We were actually a hugely talented congregation. I was allowed to preach regularly at both the English speaking and Swahili speaking services; Jim was allowed to lead services, and the students would often read the lessons, teach the congregation new songs, and eventually lead services and preach. A few months later Pastor Mtowe (Paul) was assigned by the bishop

---

[39] Mzungu is Swahili for foreigner.

Fig. 8. The author preaching at St. Margaret's Church.

to be our new pastor until a foreigner could be found to come out to Tanzania to do the job. He had been the one who had dreamt of having a healing ministry coming out of St Margaret's Church.

From then on both Pastor Mtowe and I regularly preached about healing (Fig. 8). It wasn't popular with most of the English-speaking congregation at first, but as they saw more and more people healed they gradually came round and were more positive. One man remembered a family dinner party when his father said to him, "You know, you were a horrible little boy." As he was prayed for he remembered that party, but this time he saw Jesus standing next to him and saying to his father, "I don't agree with you. I like him." It only took a few minutes but it changed that man's perception of himself.

Quite soon people began to come to the church asking for prayer for healing. One Sunday a man from Musoma (more than 350 miles away) came up to Pastor Mtowe at the end of the service and asked if there was anybody in the church who could pray for his wife who was an inpatient at KCMC. The two pastors (from the Swahili and English congregations) and I prayed for him and asked him to bring his wife down to the church the following Wednesday afternoon at 5pm so that we could pray with her personally. She duly came. The story was that she had had pain in the right upper part of her abdomen for five years. She had been to see many doctors and had been to the consultant hospital in Mwanza, but no one had been able to help her. She had been referred to KCMC as a last resort. As soon as we began to pray for her she manifested demons. We commanded them to leave in Jesus' name and they left. She went back to KCMC and had many tests done to try to find the cause of her pain. Three weeks later the couple again came to the church to give thanks that she was now well and to say that they were travelling home on the bus later that day. She showed us the letter that the hospital had given her to take back to Musoma with her. It described all the tests that she had had done - blood tests and X-rays – all of which were normal. Not surprising really as demons do not show up on blood tests and X-rays. She had not been given any treatment but she was going home well. We prayed for them again and sent them on their way with God's blessing.

A Tanzanian young man who helped me with the albino project came asking for prayer one Sunday. He was always anxious about his future and had frequent bouts of abdominal pain. His abdominal pain was instantly healed and he said, "Thank you for introducing me to THE GOD!!" The next time I saw him at work he asked me if I could give him an English Bible, which of course I did.

Another Sunday, Jeremiah, the pastor from the church in Pasua on the outskirts of Moshi, walked the four miles to St. Margaret's after his own morning service to ask for prayer for his asthma. We prayed for him and anointed him with oil. Two months later he invited Paul and me to visit him at his own church to pray again. It was a Wednesday evening.

I had got home from work at 5.45 pm after a very busy clinic, which had started at 8 am. As soon as I got home Jim drove me to Paul's house and then on to Jeremiah's church. Not only did Jeremiah want praying for, for his chest, but also his wife with upper abdominal pain, his son with a stammer, and one of the elders of the church – a lady called Pamilla – with pain down the left side of her body and decreased strength on that side.

It was all very formal to begin with. Pastor Jeremiah had put out some kneelers and I was supposed to sit behind a desk to supervise the proceedings! We started with a hymn, "All hail the power of Jesus' name," in Swahili. Pastor Mtowe told me I could sing it in English or tongues, but since he gave me a hymnbook I was able to sing in Swahili with the others. Then I had to give a talk - some words of encouragement before the prayer. I talked about Jesus being the same now as when He was on earth and us not receiving because we don't ask. Then came the praying. Pastor Mtowe told me to pray and he would translate, but for each of them we began by asking the Holy Spirit to come. When we'd finished Jeremiah said his chest felt OK, although he still had a cough. Halfway through the evening the mosquitoes came "en masse." They swarmed all over us and I found it difficult to concentrate on praying and difficult to stand still. I just wanted to scratch like crazy.

After we prayed for Jeremiah we sang another hymn and in the middle of that, the electricity went off. Jeremiah got up to light a lamp but he couldn't find a lamp in the dark and he only had one match, so we had to continue in the dark. His wife, Mariam, was next. Pastor Mtowe asked me to invite the Holy Spirit to come and then he told me to put my hand on her stomach where the pain was and he would put his hands on her head and pray. Then we prayed for Pamilla. Again I was asked to pray and he would translate. I thought the illness was due to demons so told them to go in Jesus' name. I then asked God to send His Holy Spirit to fill her so there would be no room for the demons to return. After a while she asked if she could sit down. Of course it was pitch black, we couldn't see what we were doing; but afterwards she said that she was trembling all over and initially was scared, but felt that some kind of darkness had left her and that she now felt wonderful. Then we prayed briefly for Johanna, the pastor's son, in absentia. Then the Lord's Prayer and another prayer (in Swahili). All the while, the mozzies were busy biting; only once the lights went out we couldn't see them, just hear them and feel them. We finished at 8:30 pm. Jim (who'd patiently sat outside in the Land Rover with the windows and doors shut to keep the mozzies out) then drove Pastor Mtowe back home, and then drove us home. Although we were in darkness at home too we heated up our supper on the oil stove and ate. Amazingly when we got home all the tiredness and stress of the day had completely gone and I felt wonderfully refreshed.

One Sunday morning the Swahili pastor asked us if we could pray for his wife who had a problem with her stomach. We went to the house and Pastor Mtowe, on hearing what the problem was, said "Pole sana!"[40] Afterwards I kidded him that that wasn't the kind of thing that Jesus would have said.

When we'd been in Tanzania for two years I read David Watson's book, "I believe in evangelism." One of the paragraphs that struck me was, *"The first century Christians astonished the world by their outstanding generosity even though many of them were desperately poor; by their practical care of widows and orphans, the sick and infirm; by their generous hospitality to Christian travellers. They were known for their sexual purity, for their hatred of cruelty and injustice, for their obedience to civic authorities and for their good citizenship. They were sorrowful, yet always rejoicing; they were poor, yet made many rich; they had nothing, yet they possessed everything. Here was the Spirit of Christ speaking volumes through the united witness of God's people. Today*

---

[40] Pole sana means, "I'm so sorry," or "I'm very sorry."

there are countless people with little or no sense of belonging: they are lonely and lost, searching for significance, and confused in a world that is falling apart. In this situation, the church will be highly relevant if, and only if, it becomes a genuinely caring community of love."[41] St. Margaret's was such a community for us.

We had gone out to Tanzania as volunteers. We had no income but we had to live and pay the people who worked for us. One Sunday as we were having a cup of tea after the service, an English lady who was a long-standing member of the congregation, told us about a wonderful holiday she had just been on with her husband and two children. Apparently they had stayed at a new guesthouse in Tanga (on the coast), which had only cost them 100,000 Tanzanian shillings[42] a week each. I said, "Each!" "Yes," she said. She said she thought it was very reasonable. I gulped and said that I thought it was very expensive. The only hotel we had ever stayed in had cost us £4/night for the two of us. It was just a conversation. Later that day some friends came to our house bringing an envelope from the lady we had spoken to in church that morning. Inside the envelope was a note saying, "Dear Barbara, we would like you to get a good holiday. Here are a few pounds to splash out if you get the chance. Much love, J & J." Enclosed was a cheque for £300! I cried when I opened it and saw it as a sign of God's love and provision for us. Indeed, we were wonderfully provided for in every way throughout our time in Tanzania.

---

[41] David Watson. *I believe in evangelism*, 1976, Hodder and Stoughton, p. 137-138.
[42] At that time 100,000 Tanzanian shillings was worth about £200.

CHAPTER 8
BIBLE STUDY GROUP

I no longer call you servants, because a servant does
not know his master's business. Instead I have called
you friends, for everything that I learned from my
Father I have made known to you.
John 15:15 NIV

Some of the dermatology students, like us, were worshipping at the English service at St. Margaret's Church. I wondered if they found the services as dull as I did, so after our first Christmas in Moshi I asked them if they would like to come to a Bible study in our home once a week. They said they would, and the Thursday night Bible study began in January 1993 and continued without a break for the next nine years. The first week 10 students turned up (dermatology, orthopaedic technology and nursing students from 5 different African countries). Each week we began by sharing what we thought God had been saying to us in the previous week. We then had a time of worship followed by a Bible study and we ended the evening by praying for one another. As we shared together week after week, we began to realise just how precious each one of us was to God. After all, if He took the time to speak to us, we must be important to Him. It was amazing how often He seemed to be saying the same thing to all of us.

To help us worship we used some audiocassettes from the Vineyard Church in America. They are old hat now, but at the time they were amazingly powerful in leading us into God's presence. Some weeks God was so tangibly present that all we could do was bow down or lie face down on the floor in His presence. On a few occasions a student would be terrified when that happened and run out of the house. I would then stop at a suitable point and explain what had happened. I talked about it being scary when God comes, and that we have to make a decision about whether we want to be safe or whether we're willing to do what God says. Soon the students were borrowing the tapes so that they could learn the songs and even students not coming to the Bible study were singing them. The group was great fun and I wouldn't have missed it for anything.

I taught them how to pray for the sick and how to use spiritual gifts in their everyday lives in the same way that I taught dermatology to the students at the RDTC. I taught them the theory by looking at what the Bible says. Then I demonstrated how to do it. Then I got them to do it with me watching, and then I let them loose to do it on their own. The method of praying that we used was John Wimber's five-step method of prayer[43] that I had first seen when I was on sabbatical in 1984. We practised on each other week after week. To begin with no one took any notice of what they had been taught and prayed the way they had always prayed in the past. But we always had a feedback session afterwards so that we could see where we had gone wrong. I remember one evening when Vicky (a student nurse) had been prayed for. In the feedback time afterwards she said that those praying for her had talked non-stop, leaving her no time to engage with God. That kind of feedback made me think that probably that's what Jesus did with his disciples. I can imagine Thomas saying to Jesus, "Why did you spit on the ground and then rub the mud on his eyes?"[44] It was really thrilling to see God at work in a tangible way and really exciting seeing these students longing to learn more of God and be obedient to him.

---

[43] John Wimber with Kevin Springer. *Power Healing*, 1986, Hodder and Stoughton, p. 208-244.
[44] John 9:6 (NIV).

On another evening we prayed Ephesians 1:17 over one another, "*I keep asking that the God of our Lord Jesus Christ, the glorious Father, may give you the Spirit of wisdom and revelation, so that you may know Him better.*" The following week two of the students said that they couldn't put their Bibles down; they just wanted to read it all the time! Soon they were meeting at least two other evenings a week in one of the student hostels to worship together and pray for one another. They would also go and pray for any of the other students who were sick, and occasionally would come and ask me if I would join them.

After the end of year exams in July 1993 and before some of the students went home to visit their families I thought it would be good for us to have a communion meal together. Being an Anglican I knew that you have to have a pastor who is ordained to consecrate the bread and wine for Holy Communion, so who could I ask? The Tanzanian pastor at St Margaret's had moved away to become a bishop in the far north east of the country, but there was a young pastor heading up the Swahili congregation so I went to ask him. It turned out that he couldn't help us because he was only a deacon.[45] He said that he knew a pastor who might help us and he sent one of his children to show us the way to his house. When I got there I found that the pastor had been sick for three weeks and was in fact in bed ill. His wife went and told him that he had a visitor and he got up and dressed and came out to see me. Until that moment I had no idea that I had gone to visit the man who had spoken to me after the service on the Day of Pentecost asking if I might be the mzungu to head up a healing ministry coming out of St. Margaret's. It was Pastor Paul Mtowe. I told him about the Bible study group and that I had been hoping to have a communion meal with the students before they went off home for the summer. He said that he was

---

[45] A deacon is someone who is in their first year after ordination and not yet licensed to consecrate the bread and wine for Holy Communion.

willing to help us but he couldn't at the moment because he was sick. I offered to pray with him and did so there and then. That was on the Tuesday afternoon. I didn't know if he would be able to come two days later but I decided that the group would have a meal together even if we couldn't have Holy Communion. Two days later I got home from work at 5.15 pm to find him waiting outside my house. The students all came and we had our first communion meal together. After that Paul joined the Bible study group and after a while we began to go out with him on Sundays to local village churches all over the Kilimanjaro region.[46]

Paul was a great asset to the group and gradually a few other people who weren't students also joined us, including Paul's neighbour, a Pentecostal pastor called Goodluck, and his wife Blandina, and a couple of teachers, Ada and Godwin, who were great pray-ers and great at leading worship. Nevertheless it remained primarily a student group. At the end of each evening when we prayed for one another, I would throw a foam cushion from a chair into the middle of the room and whoever wanted prayer would kneel on the cushion and the others would gather round and pray. One week when I asked who wanted prayer, Paul said, "Me!" and when I said who wants to be first he said, "Me!" He wanted to receive the gift of tongues and he was determined not to miss out on what God had for him that night. It was a real privilege to see him repent of wanting to be in control and wanting to know what he was saying when he prayed. He said in the past he had once or twice caught himself wanting to say some "peculiar" words but thought it was just silly. His humility showed me what a long way I had to go.

At about that time I re-read Helen Roseveare's book, "Give me this mountain." In it she wrote, "*In the first month that I was in the Congo, Jack Scholes (a senior missionary) drove*

---

[46] See Chapters 10 - 12.

me to a village about 12 miles off the main road. As we went he talked to me about mission ways, of the Lord's dealings, of the possibilities of success as a missionary. He said, 'If you think you have come to the mission field because you are a little better than others, or as the cream of your church, or because of your medical degrees, or for the service you can render the African church, or even for the souls you may see saved, you will fail. Remember the Lord has only one purpose ultimately for each one of us, to make us more like Jesus. He is interested in your relationship with himself. Let him take you and mould you as he will; all the rest will then take its rightful place.'"[47] Yes, I had a long way to go!

Before long Paul began to bring neighbours and friends who were sick along on a Thursday evening so they could be prayed for. One week he brought a 9-year-old boy and his mother. The boy had had a febrile fit when he was 3 years old and his mother had been worried ever since that he'd have more. For the previous eight months, Ricky (the boy) had been having abnormal movements during the night and was completely lethargic all the time. As we prayed Paul felt that Ricky might have a problem with one of his teachers at school. So we asked him if that was true. He said one of the teachers at the school had upset him very much by always giving him lower marks than he should have got. He said he wanted to fight the teacher and beat her up. The teacher's son was in the same class and she always gave her son higher marks than Ricky even though the son wasn't nearly as clever as Ricky. We talked to Ricky about Jesus healing the sick and liking children to come to him.[48] Then we prayed for him, asking God to heal him, to release him from the bondage of hatred, and to heal the disappointment and hurt from the teacher's actions. We then anointed him with oil. He came back the

---

[47] Helen Roseveare. *Give me this mountain*, 1966, Inter-Varsity Fellowship, p. 80.
[48] James 5:13-16a and Mark 10:13-16.

following Thursday completely well and full of energy. While we were praying for him (in English), his mother, Auria (who didn't speak any English), began to cry. So when we'd finished with Ricky we prayed for her. I asked her what she wanted Jesus to do for her and she replied, "I want to give my life to Him!" I got Paul to explain to her in Swahili what Jesus had done for her on the cross and then asked her to ask His forgiveness for all that she had done wrong. I then pronounced forgiveness on her and prayed for her to be filled with the Holy Spirit.

A few weeks later Auria brought her younger sister Grace who was obviously demonised. As she came from the car to the house she couldn't really walk and had to be carried into the house. Her face was grimacing and she was drooling out of the side of her mouth. I wasn't sure what to do, so decided (since Paul didn't seem to want to take the initiative) to start with worship. I prayed first and bound the evil spirits and then we worshipped. God's presence seemed to come and envelop us as we sang. One of the students led the Bible study. Grace grimaced and let out a few choice words when the name of Jesus was mentioned but it wasn't too intrusive. At the end of the study we prayed for her. Initially the demons put up a fight and said they didn't want to go, so Paul walked behind her and poured anointing oil on her head and asked the Holy Spirit to come. At this the demons were obviously terrified and she then slumped down on the settee. We sang "Baba naabudu"[49] and "Damu ya Yesu"[50] and then prayed again. She was then perfectly OK, and I took some photos of her looking very happy (Fig. 9). Apparently she'd been unwell for 9 years. I heard later that all her neighbours were asking what had happened to her, as she was so completely different. A few weeks after that Ricky brought his younger brother to the

---

[49] Father I adore you.

[50] "Damu ya Yesu usafisha kabisa" means "The blood of Jesus cleanses you completely."

group and asked us to pray for him because he was sick.

Not everyone who came to the group wanted to be prayed for. One Thursday evening a friend of Paul's turned up in the middle of the evening with an American missionary couple. The wife had terrible asthma. I offered for her to come in and be prayed for, but she wanted to see a doctor. Fortunately I found one of the physicians from KCMC at home, and although he wasn't on duty, he came to see her and sorted her out. Paul's friend who had brought her came round the next evening to say "thank you" and to say that they were very impressed with the care she had received.

Fig. 9. Grace, after she had been prayed for. She had been sick for 9 years.

On another occasion Paul brought one of his neighbours who wanted prayer for her son who was in prison. One month later we heard that he had been released from prison without being charged. Another evening he brought a theological student from Sierra Leone and his wife because the wife was sick. We prayed for her and then the husband confessed that he had a problem with alcohol and wanted to be set free from his addiction. Ada and Godwin often brought teachers from their school who had problems, and one night brought one of their neighbours who had a skin condition. Actually it was something that I could easily have treated as a doctor, but they said she wanted to be prayed for, not to see a doctor! So we prayed. Three weeks later she came back to the group to give thanks. Her skin problem had been completely healed, and never came back. Another lady who worked as a housekeeper at a local school brought a 10-year old boy who was an orphan to the group. He said that he had a problem with wetting the bed. We prayed for him and the following week he came back saying that he had only wet the bed once during the whole week, which he was thrilled about. We prayed again and he returned a month later having been completely dry for the whole month. When we came to the prayer time at the end of that evening, he was the first to ask for prayer. He said, "Please can you pray that when I go to church on Sunday I won't forget how wonderful God is!" I saw him again, by chance, four months later and he wanted to give me his Coca Cola to say thank you. He was still rejoicing over God's goodness to him.

Occasionally Pastor Mtowe asked the group to meet at his house instead of mine when he wanted us to pray for neighbours who couldn't come to the group. One evening we walked round to a neighbour's house to see a little girl who was quadriplegic after having had meningitis as a baby. We prayed for her and anointed her with oil. A week later we heard that she was moving both arms, that her legs were straightening, that she no longer cried when she was turned, and that on one occasion when she was lying down she tried to get up by herself - something she had never done before. Four months later we heard that she could now sit up on her own, that her back had straightened, that she was able to grasp things and scratch. Her legs were still bent at the knees although they were a bit straighter. The same evening that we prayed for this little girl we also prayed for another neighbour, a lady in her 50s with pain in her back. She was a widow and could no longer carry a bucket of water from the river back home. This was a problem for her as she had no one to do it for her. It turned out that she had had breast cancer some years previously, and as we prayed for her it became obvious that she was afraid that the cancer had returned and was now in her spine. We prayed telling the fear to go. A week later we found out that she was no longer afraid and was able to carry half a bucket of water on her head.

It was such an amazing privilege to be a part of that Bible study group. No two weeks were ever the same. From the moment we arrived in Tanzania I had felt completely at home. I never thought of myself as a foreigner, but one night as I was lying in bed after the Bible study group, the thought suddenly came into my head that I was the only member of the group with a white face (Fig. 10). I've no idea why I suddenly thought that, but the following week I told the group in the sharing time. They said that they never thought about it either, that I was completely accepted as being the same as them.

The same thing happened again one Sunday when I went with Vicky to Jeremiah's church on the outskirts of Moshi. We got there a little bit late and sat at the back. Halfway through the service Jeremiah called us up to the front to speak to the congregation. We hadn't introduced ourselves during

Fig. 10. The core members of the Bible study group at the beginning. From left to right, Paul Mtowe (from Tanzania), Micah (dermatology student from Kenya), Vicky (nursing student from Kenya), Harry (dermatology student from Malawi), the author (from UK), Yvonne (dermatology student from Namibia), Goma (orthopaedic technology student from Zambia).

the notices because we didn't feel like we were newcomers. Jeremiah asked me to speak and told Vicky she could translate. So I told them about us going to Lang'ata[51] and God working in people's lives – casting out demons, healing the sick, forgiving sins and enabling people to forgive those who had hurt them. I told them how thrilled we were to see God's willingness to come and touch people's lives and how we had come to worship Him with them this morning. When it came to the sermon, Jeremiah told Vicky to translate for me. When we got back to our seats I said to Vicky, "How did he know we were here?" She said, "You're the only person here with a white face!" It hadn't occurred to me.

We had a number of elective students from all over the world doing electives at KCMC, and many of them came to the Bible study group. One of them, a girl from St Bartholomew's hospital in London, wrote a nice letter when she got home thanking me for arranging for her to come to KCMC. She also wrote, "From a spiritual point of view I know it was just where God wanted me to be. I now see that it was a time He specially set aside to allow things in my heart to surface and be dealt with and a time where my faith has grown stronger. I came back with a fresh vision of the power of prayer and hope that in my own life I will take hold of the many blessings which God gave me in Tanzania and use them as a channel for God's purposes in my life. Do send my love and prayers to the Bible study group. My prayer is that you will continue to be sensitive to the leading of the Holy Spirit so that God's forgiveness, healing and power may be released to many thousands of people as they hear and receive His message."

One Thursday in September 1994 I developed pain in the left side of my back and I was a bit stiff. During the night the pain got a lot worse and I found that there was no comfortable position to lie in: I didn't get a lot of sleep. The next morning

---

[51] See Chapter 11.

I had difficulty in manoeuvring myself out of bed. Jim prayed for me and I asked him to let Paul know what had happened. The whole day was pretty awful. I tried taking paracetamol and Distalgesic, but neither made any difference to the pain. I couldn't find a position that I was comfortable in – lying, sitting, or standing – they all hurt just as much. Mid-afternoon one of the orthopaedic consultants came to the house to see me. After examining me he said that he didn't know what was wrong with me but he was pretty sure it wasn't a disc. He prescribed some Valium and told me to rest.

At about 7.30 pm Paul, Ada and Godwin all turned up to pray for me. I had been sure the whole thing was enemy action and that at a word from them it would go, but the pain was just the same when they'd finished. Godwin read me the story of the Centurion's servant from Luke's Gospel.

When Jesus had finished saying all this in the hearing of the people, he entered Capernaum. There a centurion's servant, whom his master valued highly, was sick and about to die. The centurion heard of Jesus and sent some elders of the Jews to him, asking him to come and heal his servant. When they came to Jesus, they pleaded earnestly with him, "This man deserves to have you do this, because he loves our nation and has built our synagogue." So Jesus went with them.

He was not far from the house when the centurion sent friends to say to him: "Lord, don't trouble yourself, for I do not deserve to have you come under my roof. That is why I did not even consider myself worthy to come to you. But say the word, and my servant will be healed. For I myself am a man under authority, with soldiers under me. I tell this one, 'Go,' and he goes; and that one, 'Come,' and he comes. I say to my servant, 'Do this,' and he does it."

When Jesus heard this, He was amazed at him, and turning to the crowd following him, He said, "I tell you, I have not found such great faith even in Israel." Then the men who had been sent returned to the house and found the servant well (Luke 7:1-10).

It seemed an odd passage of Scripture for him to choose, but it was an encouraging one and I expected to soon get well. When they left I went to bed and took two soluble aspirin and 10 mg of Valium. I slept nearly all night on the Friday, all day Saturday and all Saturday night. I continued taking the painkillers and Valium regularly and they made the pain bearable, although still very uncomfortable. The following Thursday, when the pain had been there unrelentingly for a week, I lay in bed thinking about the story of the Centurion's servant that Godwin had brought.

I had puzzled about it all week because, firstly Jesus didn't go to him, only gave the command, and secondly the servant got well. But as I looked at the story over and over the thing that struck me was what it said in v.4, *"this man deserves to have you do this because he loves our nation."* And it was as if God said to me that He was pleased that I loved Tanzania and the Tanzanian people.

The Bible study group came round that Thursday evening and I got out of bed and joined them. I asked Godwin why he'd read me the story of the Centurion's servant the previous week. He said he didn't know, but he thought God gave it to him so he'd just said it out of obedience. Paul said, "He read it because it says in v.4, *'this man loves our country'* and you love our country!" They prayed for me again. When they had finished praying, Paul said to me, "You are healed." I said, "I'm not, my back still hurts." He said again, "You are healed."

That night I slept well and got up on the Friday morning free of pain and I stayed pain free from then on. At 4.30 pm Henning came to the house bringing a fax for Jim, which said "URGENT." It was from Mick Arthur, the professor of medicine in Southampton, saying that my father was in hospital, jaundiced due to a blocked bile duct, and asking me to phone him after 8.30 pm that night when he would get back from a meeting in London. I thought it sounded as if dad had cancer of the head of the pancreas, but there was nothing I could do until 10.30 pm (Tanzania was two hours ahead of

UK time). At that time Henning was one of only two people we knew in Moshi who had a telephone, so I arranged to go to his house at 10.30 pm that night to phone Mick Arthur. He told me that dad had a tumour in the second part of his duodenum, obstructing the bile ducts and causing a very tight stricture of the duodenum itself, and that he had secondaries in both lungs. He talked to me about the various options and said that their immediate plan was to put in a metal stent to relieve the jaundice and take a chance on the bowel obstruction. I then rang my stepmother, Grace, to see how she was coping. Not well.

It was all amazing timing. After a week in bed unable to move, I was at least up and about and physically able to get on a plane. I wrote in my diary that night. "I guess I'll have to go home to see what is happening whatever stage dad is at and it sounds like poor Grace is at the end of her tether. Strange, I was having such a good day until the fax came. But I know that God is in control and although Satan is doing his best to jigger up the works all round, God is much more powerful than he is."

The next day I managed to get on a flight back to the UK, arriving in Southampton on Sunday morning. I found my dad to be very yellow, tired and frail, but not looking as if he was about to peg out at any moment. He wouldn't talk about his illness and said, "This is my last day at home and I want to enjoy it" (he'd been let out of hospital just for the weekend).

Once he was back in hospital I was able to sit down with him and Grace and tell him what the problem was and what was going to happen to him. All three of us cried. I was able to be with him when he had the stent put through his blocked bile duct, whenever decisions had to be made, and later when the consultant from the local hospice came to visit him at home. Once he was back home I talked to him about making his peace with God and about forgiving those who had hurt him. We talked about there being nothing between the two of us, but that he needed to forgive my brother and his wife.

I told him that God was real and that He loved him. I told him that was true and that he needed to know it for a fact. He lived for another four months and Grace took care of him at home. Three months after he died Grace came out to Tanzania to stay with us for a while.

CHAPTER 9
PRAYING IN THE HOSPITAL

*Jesus said, "I tell you the truth, the Son can do nothing
by himself; he can only do what he sees his Father doing.*
John 5:19 NIV

KCMC is a Christian hospital, set up in 1971 by The Good
Samaritan Foundation. According to its mission statement it
has three aims:-

- To render God's healing services to set mankind free
  from the bondage of sickness, suffering and sin.
- To reflect Christ's character of love, mercy, compassion
  and faithfulness in fulfilling the call to care for and heal
  the sick.
- To share God's grace and love through the power of
  the Holy Spirit in the course of treating and caring for
  the sick.

That sounds good doesn't it? Completely holistic care, given
by people who are motivated by the love of God. The reality,
though, was very different with the level of care far below
what you would expect in an NHS hospital in the UK. The
nursing care in particular was poor and I found myself getting
very angry almost every day when I found that patients had
not been given the treatment they were written up for. One
day I found a man lying helplessly on the floor having been
incontinent of faeces. When I went to ask a nurse to help me
get him up off the floor and to clean him up, I was told that he
could do it himself! Absolutely heart breaking! What would
Jesus do in such a situation? I made myself very unpopular by

insisting on having some help, but I found it hard having to complain about things like that every day.

Quite a lot of elective students came to KCMC from all over the world. I remember a German medical student who came to the Bible study group one Thursday in great distress and asking for prayer. She had thought that she had been coming to a Christian hospital and had been very upset by what she had seen on the wards. I talked to her about the Kingdom of God being the place where Jesus is King and that because He was ruling in her life, wherever she was she would bring Jesus and make a difference. Interestingly at the end of her three-month elective she came back to tell us some of the stories of God's provision for her in Tanzania and asking for more prayer. This time, that when she went home to Germany she would continue to rely on God as she had had to do in Tanzania!

Three years after I arrived at KCMC there was a new matron; a Tanzanian lady who had done her nursing training in the UK. Within weeks, all the foam mattresses on the beds were covered with plastic so they could be cleaned, and every bed had a mosquito net over it. Progress!

The RDTC sent two senior nurses to Oxford for three months to see how to run a dermatology ward. When they returned to KCMC their attitudes were completely different but initially those in authority would not let them work solely on the dermatology ward, saying that it wasn't fair that "such highly trained nurses" should only be of benefit to the patients with skin diseases. Never mind that the International Foundation for Dermatology (IFD) had paid for them to go to the UK. Later the IFD also paid for a surgical registrar to go to Oxford to be trained in plastic surgery, but when he returned we were never able to use him to operate on our albino patients.

The hospital employed a Lutheran, an Anglican and a Roman Catholic chaplain and every working day began at 7 am with a service in the chapel. Outwardly it was a Christian hospital, which meant that it was never a problem to pray with patients. I tried to behave just as I had in Southampton, signing on with my heavenly Father each day and asking Him to show me what to do. If He said to pray with a patient then I would. Otherwise I would practice conventional medicine, hopefully inspired by the love of God.

I prayed with lots of patients on the ward over the years. An old man, called Zebadayo, had an enormously swollen right hand due to Kaposi's sarcoma[52] and abdominal pain, probably due to Kaposi's sarcoma involving his gut. He lay in bed complaining bitterly about the pain in both places for two weeks without us being able to help him in any way. In the end I told him that medically we'd done all we could and that prayer was all that was left. He was happy to agree to being prayed for. Two days later he was radiant, saying that the pain had all gone and demanding to be allowed home. The man in the next bed, a Mr Kweka, had terrible eczema all over and was scratching himself uncontrollably day and night (Fig. 11). Zebadayo asked me to pray for him also, and we

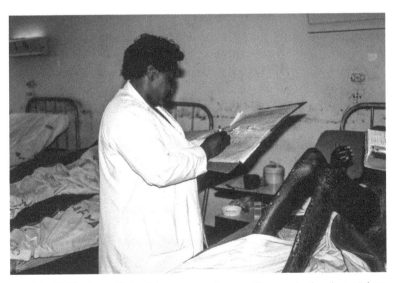

Fig. 11. Mr Kweka with terrible eczema. Yvonne Siyongo is the dermatology student writing up his treatment.

---

[52] A vascular tumour associated with AIDS.

prayed together. The next day Mr Kweka was still complaining bitterly about the itching, but he wasn't scratching all the time like he usually was. I told Zebadayo to go on praying for him. A few days later Mr Kweka was very dramatically better. He was lying in bed looking serene and peaceful and not scratching at all.

At about the same time there was a lady on the ward with mycosis fungoides, a type of lymphoma, which can cause large ulcerating tumours on the skin. She had a very large tumour behind her right ear and we planned to send her to the cancer hospital in Dar-es-Salaam for radiotherapy. She was very much afraid having been told that she had a type of cancer, so we prayed that the fear would go. The next day on my ward round, she greeted me with, "I'm still sick!" But she went on to say that all the fear had gone. She went off and had some radiotherapy to her tumour and it melted away. A year later she returned with her back covered with tumours. We prayed again and a couple of weeks later all the tumours had disappeared. I wrote in my diary, "I can only imagine that God has healed her because we haven't given her any treatment."

Very often patients would ask for prayer. The mother of a 12-year-old girl with pemphigus asked me if I could pray for her daughter. She had been in the ward for more than a month and large doses of steroids had not helped her at all. I asked one of the students to come with me to pray and all the other patients in the female ward gathered round, bowed their heads, and joined in.

On another occasion Mr Lyimo, who helped me with the albino clinic, came and asked me if I would go to one of the paediatric wards to pray for his sister's child. When I got there I found that she had had an operation the day before. Then the child's mother said she needed prayer, so I prayed for her too. Then there was another child in the same room that Mr Lyimo said wanted prayer. When I asked the child's mother she said, "Yes, she wanted prayer for her child," so I prayed. I don't know what happened to any of these people, but God knows. Certainly when people came to Jesus asking for healing, he didn't turn them away.

One day after the ward round, as I was leaving the ward with the students, a lady accosted me by name. I took one of the students with me to talk to her. It turned out she had breast cancer and wanted to know if I had any pills I could give her to cure her. The student said, "Professor, you are notorious throughout East Africa!" Apparently the lady knew a man who had been given methotrexate for his psoriasis and was clear after having problems for more than twenty years; he had suggested she come to see me!

On another occasion I was on my way to visit a lady on the obstetric ward when I met Pastor Mtowe on the stairs. He was on his way to visit his neighbour's wife. She had just delivered a dead child but there was some difficulty in delivering the placenta. We went together and prayed for her and I found myself weeping as I prayed. Within 15 minutes the placenta had been delivered and when her husband arrived a short time later she was sitting up in bed eating porridge.

Sometimes when I felt God was asking me to pray I really didn't want to. Once a year in January some senior dermatologists from around the world came to visit the RDTC to see how we were doing. One Wednesday morning the Professor of Dermatology from Oxford was observing what went on in the clinic. An old man was brought in on a stretcher and I went to see him. He had a gangrenous foot and would need an amputation. I didn't want to tell him that straight out so I told him that that he needed to come into hospital for treatment. I thought that after a few days he would be begging me to cut his leg off because the pain was so bad. But to my surprise he said that he did not want to come into hospital. Just at that moment I felt God prompting me to offer to pray for him. I was very conscious of the Professor from Oxford (a world expert on vascular problems) standing only six feet away. I changed from speaking English to the man to Swahili and asked him if he knew Jesus?

"Yes."

"Did he love Jesus?"

"Yes."

"Shall we ask Jesus to heal you?"

"Yes."

So I put one hand on the offending leg and, again in Swahili, asked Jesus to heal him. I had nothing more to offer so away he went on his stretcher. I wrote in his notes, "Gangrenous right foot. PRAY." And signed my name. Three weeks later an elderly man walked in to the clinic accompanied by his daughter. I didn't recognise him, but when I opened his notes I saw in my own handwriting, "Gangrenous right foot. PRAY." I asked him to show me his foot and it was completely normal! I asked his daughter why they had come back and she said, "We wanted to check that he was alright!" Actually I think that God was being really kind to me because I really hadn't wanted to pray in front of the Professor from Oxford.

On another occasion I was walking back from the Grand Round one Wednesday morning, when someone accosted me and asked if I would pray for a lady outside Casualty. Just as I got there I saw Goma (a Zambian student from the Bible study group) walking by so I asked him if he would come and pray with me. The lady didn't speak any English so neither Goma nor I had any idea what was wrong with her. We laid hands on her and prayed as she sat on the bench under the tree outside Casualty. All the doctors and students going back to the hospital from the Grand Round turned to stare at us as we prayed. A year later we heard that she had just delivered a baby boy, and that the problem had been that she couldn't get pregnant.

If we want to do what the Father is doing[53] we need to understand that He knows best and go with it, even if we feel uncomfortable. John Wimber used to say that faith is spelt

---

[53] John 5:19 (NIV).

RISK and indeed it is. Was it worth the embarrassment to see an old man walk and be pain free instead of having his leg cut off? Was it worth the embarrassment to see a woman who would have been discarded by her husband and sent home to her parents in shame, have a happy family life? The only possible answer was "YES."

In 1997 KCMC started a medical school under the newly formed Tumaini[54] University. When the first group of students arrived I was asked to teach them about "wholeness, not just physical healing." I had just been reading, "Keeping a spiritual journal," edited by Edward England, so it was timely. In the book Sister Margaret Magdalen wrote, *"It is strange how, when we are physically wounded, we will take every possible step to find healing. We are prepared to spend time sitting in the doctor's surgery or taking our turn in the long queue at A&E at the local hospital. However inconvenient, we will go immediately to the chemist for a prescription ... possibly another long wait. We know that unless we get treatment, we shall not be able to function properly in our temporary state of handicap. And in our brokenness we will submit to X-rays, plasters, pinning etc. Yet how many of us are willing to take time out to give God a chance to deal with those other wounds that are debilitating to our spiritual health .... and to our physical, emotional and mental health too for, psychosomatic beings that we are, our unhealed memories affect the whole self."*[55] I was assigned a two-hour session together with the Lutheran pastor. He started the lecture and said, "Doctors from the West always ask 'What is the cause of this illness?' We in Tanzania ask, 'Who is the cause of this illness?'" That was a complete eye opener for me. I had met people who had told me that a neighbour, or a member of the family, had put a curse on them when I had been preaching in local villages, but

---

[54] Tumaini in Swahili means hope.
[55] Sister Margaret Magdalen. *Keeping a spiritual journal*, 1988, Highland Books, p. 77-78.

I hadn't met that concept in the hospital before. Probably they simply hadn't told me because I was a foreigner.

One afternoon as I was walking from one ward to another I met one of the psychiatrists who asked me if I would see one of her patients, a young man called Tobias, who had acne. Obviously that wouldn't be a problem, but she proceeded to tell me a little bit about him. He was 20 years old, had no family and had been sleeping rough in Dar-es-Salaam. She told me that both his mother and grandfather had committed suicide, so it wasn't really surprising that he was mentally ill. As she told me that, something inside me protested vehemently and I thought, "No! Why should he be mentally ill just because other members of his family had been?" I went to see him on the ward and I found a young man who was literally just skin and bone. My first thought was that he had AIDS, and I suggested that they check his HIV status. When I found out that it was negative I invited him to come to the Bible study at my house the next day. Amazingly he turned up. When we prayed for him he immediately manifested demons, so we commanded them to leave in Jesus' name. The demons kept saying things like, "Bwana[56] we're leaving," but they didn't go. Then suddenly I was inspired to ask him to roll up his sleeve. On his upper arm he was wearing a copper bangle. I asked him what it was, and he told me that his grandfather had given it to him. I told him to take it off. He was reluctant to do so, but when Pastor Mtowe also told him to take it off, he did so. We then commanded the evil spirits to leave in the name of Jesus and they went.

When everyone had gone home I took the bangle to the bottom of the garden and threw it in the deep hole, which was our rubbish tip. The next morning I thought that having a bangle associated with evil in our back garden probably wasn't a good idea, so I went to collect it to take it elsewhere.

---

[56] Bwana in Swahili means Lord.

But it wasn't there: it had disappeared in the night. When I went to the hospital that morning Tobias came to find me. He asked for his bangle back. I told him that I had got rid of it so he couldn't have it back. He was very upset with me. I told him that Jesus was far more powerful than Satan. That it was the name of Jesus which had got rid of the demons that had been living inside him and that he needed to trust in Jesus from now on. I prayed for him again and he came to the Bible study group again the following Thursday looking absolutely radiant. He quickly put on weight and was able to be discharged from hospital. Many people in Tanzania went to witch doctors rather than to Jesus for healing – even Christians! They thought it didn't matter, but it did.

CHAPTER 10
GOING OUT TO PREACH THE GOSPEL

Then Jesus went around teaching from village to village.
Calling the Twelve to him, he sent them out two by two
and gave them authority over evil spirits.
These were his instructions: "Take nothing for the
journey except a staff - no bread, no bag, no money in
your belts. Wear sandals but not an extra tunic.
Whenever you enter a house, stay there until you
leave that town. And if any place will not welcome
you or listen to you, shake the dust off your feet
when you leave, as a testimony against them."
Mark 6:6b-12 NIV

Paul Mtowe, who had joined the Bible study group, was also the Rural Dean. That meant that on Sundays he travelled around to churches that didn't have a pastor of their own. There were many such churches in the Kilimanjaro region led by an evangelist rather than a pastor. The evangelist usually had a secular job and looked after the church in his spare time. When Paul had been part of the Bible study group for about five months he told us that he was going to Same (a town about 100 km from Moshi) on the following Sunday. He had been there several times before and was excited about the people there who had responded to prayer. He said that healing was proving to be a good way of evangelism there. I suggested that he should take the students and me with him on the Sunday and he thought that was a good idea. Normally he would have gone on the bus, but if we all went we could all go in the Land Rover together. It seemed like a good idea at the time. The only person who wasn't pleased about it was my husband. In fact he was pretty cross about it. He liked driving the Land Rover so I thought he would like the opportunity to drive us to a new place. But being an owl rather than a lark, 7 am on a Sunday morning was not the ideal time for him. I should have asked him first! Nevertheless, he agreed to take us.

We got up at 5.30 am to get ready for the day. The students turned up just after 7 am and we set off for Pastor Mtowe's house and then on to Same. Paul had told us the service started at 10 am but that we needed to be there in good time. As it turned out the service didn't start until 10.30 am. When we arrived at 9.15 am we were taken to someone's house and given tea and samosas until the service began.

The church met in a primary school classroom! It was interesting sitting behind a school desk with not enough room to stand properly. Paul introduced us as the St. Margaret's Church choir. We sang two songs at different points in the service – "I believe in Jesus" near the beginning, and "Bind us together" after the sermon during the offertory. It ended up with everyone all round the church standing up and holding hands as we sang. Paul preached about Jesus healing the sick but gave no opportunity for anyone to be prayed for.

We went back to someone's house for lunch and then various people who wanted prayer arrived one after the other. How they knew to come I never did find out. As we prayed with each one, the Holy Spirit came with some visible manifestations. Paul was like a child with a new toy: he was so excited by what God was doing. One lady, called Brigitta, wanted prayer for long-standing asthma. When we prayed for her she began to cry and covered her head with her kanga[57] so that she could cry in private. When we asked her afterwards

---

[57] A kanga is a large piece of cloth which a mother uses to strap her baby to her back (see Fig. 84). It can also be wrapped around the body as a skirt, head-wrap or apron, or used as a potholder or towel (see Figs. 1, 17, 31, 51, 87).

what had happened she said, "I've been saved!" We then prayed for her husband, Philip, who was the local evangelist! We prayed for him to be anointed for his work. The whole thing was more or less in Swahili. The students and I prayed in English and someone translated; the Swahili on the whole wasn't translated back to English for us. By the time we'd done all that it was gone 4 pm. So off we set for home.

A month later we got some feedback from Pastor Mtowe about the people at Same. Apparently Brigitta hadn't had any asthma since we prayed, Philip was beaming and another lady was very, very happy and praising God. The people there told him that our visit had made a big difference to their lives and invited us to go again.

Four months later we did go again. On that particular day Paul had bought with him three copies of the service book and three hymn books for us to share, so for the first time on one of our trips out the students and I were able to join in the songs and follow the service. It was a normal Anglican Morning Prayer service in Swahili; very formal and yet there was time for God to act.

On this visit we found that Same had now got a pastor of their own but they were still meeting in the local primary school. The students asked all the children to come out to the front to act out the story of Jesus providing breakfast for the disciples at the side of Lake Galilee. It was after the resurrection and they had been fishing all night but had caught nothing. Then when Jesus told them where to cast their net they caught a lot of fish.[58] The students also sang, Vicky gave a testimony, and I preached on the story that the children had acted out, with Paul translating (Fig. 12). I remember at one point when I stopped for him to translate, he said, "I've already told them that, move on!" It was so good working with someone who was on the same wavelength.

---

[58] John 21:1-14 (NIV).

Fig. 12. The author preaching at Same: Paul Mtowe translating.

After the sermon I called forward anyone who hadn't realised that Jesus had died for them, anyone who had kept Jesus out of their everyday lives (those who thought God was only for Sundays), and those who, when sick or in trouble, had been to witchdoctors or traditional healers instead of to the living God. Initially no one responded, but once one did many others soon followed. I got them all to repent and then pronounced forgiveness over them. We then prayed for any who were sick and after that went on to Holy Communion. While we were there, we also prayed for the new pastor and his wife who had been married for 10 years but had not been able to have children.

After the service we went back to the churchwarden's house for tea and bread (Fig. 13). We were then asked to go to the home of someone who was sick who hadn't been able to come to church. A pick-up truck came to collect us (Fig. 14) and took us to Sebastian's house. He was in bed when we got there. We waited while the family got him dressed and then he came to join us. He was an old man who was very, very thin

Fig. 13. Tea and bread together in the churchwarden's house after the service in Same.

Fig. 14. We went by pick-up truck to visit Sebastian at home.

and looked as if he was dying. He said the problem was with his stomach, so I assumed that he had some kind of bowel cancer, which had spread. Later his daughter brought out a recent chest X-ray which showed a large tumour in his left lung. We had a brief communion service for him in the house and then we prayed for him.

We then went back to the churchwarden's house for lunch. By then it was 3.30 pm. After lunch I was asked to see the churchwarden's wife, who had had problems with headaches and stomach pains for more than fourteen years. Apparently she had been prayed for once before, in 1980, but it hadn't made any difference. I read her James 5:13-16[59] and then prayed for her – laying my hands on her head and then anointing her with oil. She said that she felt tingling going through her body but I never heard what happened to her.

One Thursday night about a month later Paul announced that we would be going to two different churches the following Sunday. He and I would go to Mwanga, and the students would go to Same. Goma (an orthopaedic technician student from Zambia) would preach at Same and Vicky (a Kenyan nursing student) would translate his sermon into Swahili. I thought it would be better to divide the students in half and for Paul to be with one group and me to be with the other, but he said they didn't need us watching over them and would manage on their own. So that's what we did.

The next problem was to find a driver as Jim was going to be busy elsewhere on that Sunday. Eventually I asked a friend who was a teacher at the International School if she could drive us to both places as they were only 20 km apart. She said,

---

[59] Is anyone among you in trouble? Let them pray. Is anyone happy? Let them sing songs of praise. Is anyone among you sick? Let them call the elders of the church to pray over them and anoint them with oil in the name of the Lord. And the prayer offered in faith will make the sick person well; the Lord will raise them up. If they have sinned, they will be forgiven. Therefore confess your sins to each other and pray for each other so that you may be healed. The prayer of a righteous person is powerful and effective.

"Yes," so off we went. Paul and I were dropped off in Mwanga and the students went on to Same. When they had finished at Same they picked us up on their way home. Yvonne, one of the dermatology students recited Goma's sermon to us in the car on the way back. He had used exactly the same readings as I had, and Paul accused me (in fun) of stealing Goma's sermon and forbade us from giving the same sermon in two places at once in the future!

It sounded as if the students had had a good time. They had prayed for 5 people who wanted to be filled with the Holy Spirit and for many others who were sick. After the service they had gone to Brigitta's house and she told them that she had had no asthma since we had prayed for her 6 months earlier. They also heard that Sebastian had died a month after our visit, but had been praising God right to the end. I asked my teacher friend (our driver) how the day had gone. She said that she had enjoyed it, but that there had been a bit too much praying for her liking. She found it odd that the students prayed and gave thanks to God before they drank a Coca Cola! But it couldn't have been too bad because she said she would be prepared to drive us again – just not every week! Obviously we didn't need to keep going to Same once they had a pastor of their own. But, four years later we caught up with their pastor and his wife at a church in Moshi, only to find that they had twin daughters (Fig. 15). God is so good!

The Anglican Church in Mwanga met in one of the classrooms at the local primary school. On one occasion we got there early and were waiting in one of the classrooms for people to arrive (Fig. 16) when we heard beautiful hymn singing coming from one of the other classrooms. I asked the churchwarden who was with us, "Who is that singing?"

He replied, "They're the *'born again'* ones!" I asked him to elaborate and he said, "They're the ones who've been saved!"

I said, "Aren't you saved then?"

He said, "No, I'm not saved because I sometimes drink alcohol."

Fig. 15. The pastor from Same with his wife and 2-year old twin daughters.

Fig. 16. The church in Mwanga: waiting for the service to begin in a primary school classroom.

I tried to explain that being saved was nothing to do with drinking alcohol or not, but about accepting what Jesus had done for you on the cross. Paul touched on it again in his sermon and at the end of the service he invited me to say a few words, so I talked about it again, illustrating it from the story of Zacchaeus.[60] It was <u>after</u> Jesus had invited himself to his house for dinner that Zacchaeus changed. Jesus didn't ask him to change before he would visit him. I'm not sure that the churchwarden was convinced but many others were.

In the service we sang several songs as a group, Micah (a Kenyan dermatology student) gave a testimony, Paul preached, and then invited those who wanted to give their lives to Christ to put up their hands and then come forward. Nine did. After those who wanted to become Christians had come forward and repented and been prayed for, he then invited those who were sick to come forward for prayer. I prayed with Vicky. The first person we prayed for was a little girl aged 5, who came with her mum. I asked her mum what she wanted Jesus to do for her daughter and she said, "She can't speak." So we prayed and then the little girl said very loudly, "Mama." At the end of the service an old man came out of the classroom very happy. He couldn't stop laughing. He hugged Paul and danced around with him because he was <u>so</u> happy.

As a group we went to Mwanga on lots of occasions. It was on the way to Same, just off the main road from Moshi to Dar-es-Salaam but only 80 km away. Trips there tended to be shorter because they were closer to home. One Sunday we were on our way home, nice and early at 2.30 pm, when the Land Rover lost power. Jim pulled over to the side of the road to see what had happened, only to find that we had two flat tyres. We were 30 km from home but we only had one spare wheel with us; we had left the second one in the garage at home. Bother! Paul flagged down a passing car and spoke to

---

[60] Luke 19:1-10 (NIV).

the man and woman inside. They were on their way to Moshi and he persuaded them to take two of us with them. Paul's wife came with me, so that she could speak Swahili when needed. We were dropped off in the centre of Moshi and made our way to the nearest bus stop. As we were waiting for a bus, a Norwegian student from St. Margaret's Church was driving by in the opposite direction. He saw us and stopped and agreed to drive us home. We then got the spare wheel out of the garage and I went along to a friend, David, who lived next door-but-one to us on the doctor's compound. I asked him if he would be able to drive us, and the spare wheel back to Jim and the others? He agreed. When we got back to the stranded Land Rover it was raining. Jim had changed one wheel and the other was ready to take off with the nuts unscrewed ready, so it only took a few minutes to put on the other spare wheel. David kindly drove behind us all the way home just to make sure we didn't get another puncture. But everyone got safely home. That was one of the wonderful things about living in Africa. People would always help you out if you were in trouble, and everyone shared what they had. There was a wonderful sense of belonging together and holding all things in common.

About 20 km south of Moshi was a huge sugar cane plantation employing up to 3000 people at the height of the season. Our group was asked to go to there one Sunday, but a local evangelist had been invited to preach. I'm not sure what they were expecting us to do. But we went. When we got there we were told that the evangelist wasn't going to come after all, so Paul said I would have to preach. I looked out over a congregation of about 150 people, nearly all of whom were young adults. I remember thinking that there was no point in thinking that there would be anyone who needed healing because they all looked fit and well. Three choirs marched into the church from three different directions at the start of the service. They all had different uniforms and the whole spectacle was very colourful. I wondered what on earth I could preach about to such a group of people. I just shut my eyes and prayed that God would give me whatever words were necessary. When the time came for me to preach I decided to read the story of the man who was healed outside the temple gate from Acts chapter 3 (verses 1-10). It says,

"*One day Peter and John were going up to the temple at the time of prayer — at three in the afternoon. Now a man crippled from birth was being carried to the temple gate called Beautiful, where he was put every day to beg from those going into the temple courts. When he saw Peter and John about to enter, he asked them for money. Peter looked straight at him, as did John. Then Peter said, 'Look at us!' So the man gave them his attention, expecting to get something from them.*

Then Peter said, 'Silver or gold I do not have, but what I have I give you. In the name of Jesus Christ of Nazareth, walk.' Taking him by the right hand, he helped him up, and instantly the man's feet and ankles became strong. He jumped to his feet and began to walk. Then he went with them into the temple courts, walking and jumping, and praising God. When all the people saw him walking and praising God, they recognised him as the same man who used to sit begging at the temple gate called Beautiful, and they were filled with wonder and amazement at what had happened to him."

Then I asked them how many of them had ever done anything like that? No response. I asked them to put up their hands if they had ever done anything like that. No one did so. Then I read John 14:12 to them, where Jesus says to his disciples, "*I tell you the truth, anyone who has faith in me will do what I have been doing. He will do even greater things than these, because I am going to the Father.*" I said, "It says here that we are supposed to do these things." Then I read John 3:16 to them. "*For God so loved the world that he gave his one and only Son, that whoever believes in him shall not perish but have eternal life.*" I asked them how many of them believed that? Nearly everyone put up their hands. I re-read John 14:12 to them and asked them how many of them believed it? Again, nearly everyone put up their hands. So I said to them, "Then why don't you do it?"

Two people put their hands up to give a reason. The first lady said, "I've only just become a Christian; I didn't know you were supposed to do these things."

The second said, "I don't know Jesus so how could I do these things?"

It was so easy then to tell them about Jesus - who He is and what He came to do. No advance preparation had been needed. I then invited people to come forward if they wanted to give their lives to Christ. Four ladies came forward immediately, including the one at the beginning who'd said she didn't know Jesus and another man later in the service. They all got filled with the Holy Spirit and spoke in tongues. I then invited those who were sick to come forward (about 30 did so) and the team and the four ladies who had just become Christians prayed for them. One lady told us that she had been a Christian but after some problems with her brother-in-law had stopped going to church. Then just a week before our visit she said that God had told her to fast for seven days (she finished that day) and He would then enable her to pray for the sick! She cried a lot and then prayed aloud in tongues. Another lady had had chest pains for years and the pain went. I lost count of the number of people I prayed for. At the end we anointed all those who had come forward. Paul started at one end and I started at the other and we met somewhere around the middle. It was wonderful to see God at work. I hadn't planned on preaching that morning. I had no idea what to say and absolutely no plans until I opened my mouth. God is amazing!

We eventually got a new pastor for the English-speaking congregation at St. Margaret's Church from the UK. About three months after his arrival he joined us on a trip to Ngorika, a church on the other side of Nyumba ya Mungu from Lang'ata. It was a church that St. Margaret's were supporting. They had paid £60 for a small house to be built there for a pastor, and had in the past given money for both a pastor and an evangelist. We had never been to that church before and we got lost trying to find it. We didn't get there until 12 midday, although the service had been meant to start at 10 am. When we got there the church was empty. I thought that people had got fed up waiting for us and had gone back home, but apparently not. Someone rang the church bell and took us to someone's house to have a soda. It was lovely to sit in the cool of a house and have a cold drink after our long and somewhat tiresome journey (we had set off at 8 am). By the time we'd finished having something to drink the church was full.

The service went well. Paul decided that I would preach and there was a very good response with people wanting to be saved and healed. There was one demonised young woman, who made a lot of noise. Apparently the demons were saying, "In the name of Satan I won't come out!" But in the end she was free. It turned out she didn't live in the village and had just come that day to visit her father!

I prayed with Vicky. The first person we prayed for was a 10-year-old boy, Michael, with a chest infection. After we had prayed for him we asked his mother if she would like prayer too. She said that her husband was in prison and could we pray for him? We asked her to tell us her name and she replied, "Khadija."

That sounded like a Muslim name so I asked her if she was Muslim?

"Yes."

I told her that we could only pray in the name of Jesus, was that OK?

"Yes."

When we finished praying, she said she wanted to give her life to Christ! We explained to her about repentance. She repented of her sins and then we proclaimed God's forgiveness over her. After the service she came up and asked if she could be baptised.

The new pastor from St. Margaret's was praying with Paul's wife and they said that everyone they prayed for wanted to give their lives to Christ.

Some Sundays we went to African churches in Moshi or on the outskirts of Moshi. One of these was Jeremiah's church at Pasua. One Sunday one of the local evangelists was going to preach at Pasua, and he agreed to give us all a lift to the church. We were to meet him at the bus station but he didn't turn up so we got a taxi instead. We asked the taxi driver to come back and pick us up at 12.30 pm. Paul said I would have to preach but at 9.30 am the preacher turned up!

The service was good. It lasted from 9.30 am to 1.10 pm and we were sitting on low wooden benches. Amazingly it didn't seem long at all. Vicky translated the sermon for me. Paul introduced everyone and made me stand up and talk for a few minutes, which I did. I talked about our Bible study group meeting together to learn to do the things Jesus did, and that we should expect to do them and, like Jesus, learn to do what the Father is doing.[61] The preacher talked about healing and, after communion, Paul called anyone who wanted to be healed to come forward. About ten did, all ladies. I asked Paul to check that there were no children who were sick who needed prayer. He brought back a little girl with vitiligo.[62] Yvonne (one of the dermatology students) and I prayed for her twice, but she still had vitiligo when we'd finished praying. I then took Yvonne with me to pray for all the others. One old man came up for prayer and began shaking uncontrollably. I had the privilege of going along the row anointing some of them with oil, including the old man, Frederick. When he got up he was jumping up and down shouting, "Alleluia!" and tears were streaming down his face. I think he must have been baptised with the Holy Spirit. A young woman called Faith

---

[61] John 5:19 (NIV).

[62] Vitiligo is a skin disease where the skin loses its pigment and the skin goes white. Obviously this is a lot more noticeable in Africans than in Europeans.

had had stomach pains for months and was healed. Another young woman, Naomi, was slain in the Spirit.[63] Jeremiah called two very large ladies to come and carry her out to the vestry. I don't know why he did that.

When everyone had been prayed for, the choir sang another song. Paul then called anyone who had been healed to come forward and testify. Faith and Frederick did so; they were both bubbling over with joy about what God had done for them. We then sang another hymn and marched outside and shook hands with everyone.

We had asked the taxi driver to come back for us at 12.30 pm but we didn't get outside until about 1.10 pm and there was still the lady who had been slain in the Spirit flat out in the vestry. One of the churchwardens offered to take us home, so I paid the taxi driver for the time he had waited which meant we weren't in a hurry.

We went back in and prayed for the lady, Naomi lying on the vestry floor. Paul commanded demons to come out of her in a very stern voice and at the third attempt she stopped thrashing around and rolling all over the floor and calmed down. He then told her to get up, which she promptly did, with her back problem apparently healed! We all sat in the vestry then and were given sodas[64] to drink. For some reason I had the urge to pour the anointing oil on Paul's head, so I did! Jeremiah came in to join us a bit later. He thought Paul was sweating because the oil had run down from the top of his head onto his face and neck. I read Psalm 133[65] to them and

---

[63] Acts 9:1-8 (v. 3); Ezekiel 1:25-2:3 (v.28); Daniel 10:4-21 (v.8); Revelation 1:12-19 (v.17).

[64] Sodas were fizzy drinks like Coca Cola, Fanta, Sprite, Tangawizi and Bitter Lemon.

[65] How good and pleasant it is when brothers live together in unity! It is like precious oil poured on the head, running down on the beard, running down on Aaron's beard, down upon the collar of his robes. It is as if the dew of Hermon were falling on Mount Zion. For there the Lord bestows his blessing, even life for evermore.

they all thought it was hilarious. But I think God was in it and that Paul was blessed.

Every Sunday was different. Every Sunday was amazing. One week we went to a Lutheran church at a village called Sungu. It was quite a small church in a largely Roman Catholic area. Paul preached about Jesus healing the sick and afterwards welcomed anyone who would like to be healed to come up to the communion rail. The last lady we prayed for was a lady in her fifties called Piambe. She said that she was hearing noises and voices in her head. We prayed for her and anointed her head with oil and commanded any evil spirits to go, but not much seemed to happen. Paul and I both had the idea that we should go to her house, so after lunch we did. When we got there, it turned out that her husband had died and was buried in the garden. He had been a Roman Catholic, but had allowed his wife to attend the Lutheran Church, which was very unusual in that area. Paul prayed by the husband's graveside giving thanks for his life. He then anointed the doorpost of the house and prayed for the house. Immediately Piambe was a changed woman, beaming from ear to ear. Extraordinary! She never heard noises or voices in her head again.

CHAPTER 11
LANG'ATA

*They sailed to the region of the Gadarenes,
which is across the lake from Galilee. When Jesus
stepped ashore, He was met by a demon-possessed man
from the town. For a long time this man had not worn
clothes or lived in a house, but had lived in the tombs.
When he saw Jesus, he cried out and fell at his feet,
shouting at the top of his voice, "What do you want
with me, Jesus, Son of the Most High God? I beg you,
don't torture me!" For Jesus had commanded the
impure spirit to come out of the man. Many times it had
seized him, and though he was chained hand and
foot and kept under guard, he had broken his chains and
had been driven by the demon into solitary places.
Jesus asked him, "What is your name?" "Legion,"
he replied, because many demons had gone into him.
And they begged Jesus repeatedly not to order
them to go into the Abyss.*

*A large herd of pigs was feeding there on the hillside.
The demons begged Jesus to let them go into the pigs,
and he gave them permission. When the demons
came out of the man, they went into the pigs,
and the herd rushed down the steep bank into
the lake and was drowned.*

*When those tending the pigs saw what had happened,
they ran off and reported this in the town and
countryside, and the people went out to see what had
happened. When they came to Jesus, they found the man
from whom the demons had gone out, sitting at Jesus'
feet, dressed and in his right mind; and they were afraid.*
Luke 8:26-35 NIV

One Thursday night at the Bible study group Paul reported that he had been to a village about 50 km south of Moshi to see a woman who had been mentally ill for sixteen years. Her behaviour was very like that of the Gadarene demoniac described in Luke's Gospel. The woman, whose name was Grace, behaved in a very bizarre manner and it often took ten people to hold her down so that she could be given an injection to subdue her. She had a son who had been taken away from her as a young child because she was not able to take care of him. She had been to doctors in Tanzania, Kenya and Mozambique but seemingly no one could help her. I'm not sure how Paul got involved, but he went to Lang'ata (the name of the village where she lived) with two friends and prayed for her. They cast out many demons and just like the Gadarene demoniac she was then transformed and was able to sit quietly and in her right mind.[66]

From that day on she was well and went around telling people how wonderful Jesus was and how he had healed her. When her neighbours realised that she really was changed, they sent for her son to come home. He was now a young man in his early twenties. He didn't believe that his mother could have changed and initially refused to believe it. But he was persuaded to come and see and returned home to find his mother completely normal (Fig. 17). I saw Grace on

Fig. 17. Grace and her son Gabriel at Lang'ata.

---

[66] Luke 8:35.

Fig. 18. The journey to Lang'ata squashed in the back of the Land Rover.

many occasions over the years when we visited Lang'ata or when she travelled to Moshi to visit Paul and he brought her to visit us at home.

As a result of Grace's healing we were invited to Lang'ata to lead the service there, even though they had both a pastor and evangelist of their own. In many ways it was our first proper adventure out together as a group, and the first time that I was to preach. We set off at 8 am, eleven of us squashed into the Land Rover (Fig. 18), and although it was only 50 km from Moshi it took us more than two hours to get there cross country on small dirt roads. At one point the road was washed away and we had to turn around to find a different way (no satnavs in those days). When we got there we discovered that Lang'ata (Fig. 19) was at the side of a lake called Nyumba ya Mungu,[67] and as we approached it, it looked absolutely beautiful (Fig. 20).

---

[67] Nyumba ya Mungu means "House of God." In this case it was the name of a 140 km^2 man-made lake from which the hydroelectric power to supply Moshi and the surrounding area came.

Fig. 19. Lang'ata.

Fig. 20. Nyumba ya Mungu at Lang'ata.

When we got there the church (a proper brick built church) was empty (Figs. 21 & 22). We walked down to the lakeside just to enjoy the view and were then taken to the church office and given tea and chapattis.

Fig. 21. Outside of the church at Lang'ata.

Fig. 22. Inside of the church at Lang'ata.

Then when we went back to the church it was pretty full and there were lots and lots of children. I wondered, as I looked at the children, whether what I thought God had asked me to say was completely wrong - the stories I had planned to tell were not really appropriate for children. I had planned to teach about the healing of the woman who had been bleeding for twelve years and the raising of Jairus' daughter from the dead from Mark 5:21-43. But when it came to it, the pastor there had chosen two other readings and didn't want to change them. So at the start of my sermon I had to ask Paul to read the story from Mark's Gospel so everyone would know the story I was talking about. My basic message to them was that Jesus was the same today as when He was on earth and that He was present with them at that moment and they could bring their problems to Him.

After the sermon I asked all those who wanted their sins forgiven to come forward to the front of the church and about 30 people came forward. I told them to tell Jesus in their own words what they had done wrong and to ask his forgiveness. I then asked Paul to pronounce forgiveness over them and then I prayed for the Holy Spirit to come and fill them. I then called all those who were sick to come forward. Most of those who had come forward for forgiveness and to know Jesus stayed, and lots of others came up, including several ladies who were demonised and behaving in very bizarre ways. There was one lady running up and down the aisle with her arms in the air and shrieking. Paul told two of the students to take her to the back of the church and deal with her! I heard him tell them but I thought, "They won't know what to do!" There was lots of shrieking, someone down on all fours barking like a dog, a lady writhing on the ground like a snake, and lots of peculiar movements and lots of talking from the demons saying they wouldn't go, or let them stay until tomorrow. In the middle of all this chaotic behaviour, the pastor came up to Paul in great distress and said, "We haven't taken the collection yet!" Since his salary was what came in in the collection he was afraid he wasn't going to eat that week.

In the end the demons came out of all but one of the ladies and Paul told the local pastor what to do for them the following week. The demons absolutely refused to come out of the last lady. They kept saying things like, "Let me stay for another half an hour."

At one point Paul said in English, "Lord, send your fire down on them."

And the woman screamed out in Swahili, "Aaah, you're burning me!"

In the end Paul said to them, "I will give you half an hour. When we come back you are to have gone."

We left her lying on the floor of the church and went to the church office for lunch as by then it was gone 3 pm.

After lunch we got a message that Grace, the lady who had had the numerous demons cast out of her by Paul and his friends two months earlier, wanted us to call at her house so that she could give us a present of some pumpkins and small fish. So next stop Grace's house. When we got there she wanted us to go inside, but it was getting late and we wanted to go home. Paul told me to just go into the house and bless Grace and her home, so I went inside to do that. It was a tiny mud house (one room), which was spotlessly clean. Inside was a young woman looking very forlorn. Grace said she'd wanted to come to the church that morning but hadn't been able to make it. She had gone to Grace's house because she knew we were going there. I asked her if she knew Jesus and she said, "No, I'm a Muslim."

I said the only person who could heal her (she'd had pains in her chest for six years) was Jesus and we could only pray to Him. Would she like us to pray?

"Yes."

I asked the Holy Spirit to come and immediately she started manifesting demons. I told them to go in Jesus' name but they took absolutely no notice. She was sitting on a chair, but even so she was writhing about and shaking her head furiously. The demons wouldn't tell me their names and they wouldn't go. I sent for Paul to come and help. Again, initially nothing happened. Then Paul asked her if she had any idols in her house and she said, "Yes." So he sent someone to fetch her husband and to bring the idols to be burnt. Once that was done, the demons left without any further fight. We then sang some songs about who Jesus is and that his blood cleanses us from all sin. Then we went outside with her and proclaimed to half the village, who were standing outside, that Jesus had healed her and she was able to say, "Thank you, Jesus" and proclaim him as Lord. It was wonderful to see her transformed.

By the time we got home it was 9 pm! One of the dermatology students said, "Please don't ask me to go out with you on a Sunday again. It was too long." But before long all of the students were asking when we were going again as it had been so exciting to see God at work. Interestingly in spite of the local pastor's fears, the collection, when it was taken, was more than double the usual amount!

Two weeks later, Grace turned up at Paul's house in Moshi to tell him about some of the things that had happened in Lang'ata. Fatima, the lady we had prayed for in Grace's house, was completely healed and liberated and was praising God all the time. Amazingly her husband was allowing her to go to Grace's house every day to pray. The lady that we had left lying on the floor of the church, Mercy, was also apparently completely free and well. An old lady who had been deaf got her hearing back. A lady with hugely swollen legs due to elephantiasis was running around the village because her legs were now back to normal. A child with epilepsy had not had any more fits and another child who was *useless* was now normal and fetching water and helping in the house. She said that the following Sunday everyone was standing around outside the church talking about the wonderful things that God had done.

Fig. 23. The church at Lang'ata Magongo.

Fig. 24. Lang'ata Magongo: ringing the church bell.

Six months later we returned to Lang'ata, but we were taken to the tiny church in the next village of Lang'ata Magongo (Fig. 23). The people there said it wasn't fair for us to only go to the main church in Lang'ata. Again no one was there when we arrived, but they rang the church bell (Fig. 24) and the people came (Fig. 25). Everyone sat on low benches (Fig. 26), but they brought some chairs from the local school for our group to sit on (Fig. 27). The church was packed with children, most of them sitting on the floor

Fig. 25. Lang'ata Magongo: everyone came when the church bell had been rung.

Fig. 26. Inside the church at Lang'ata Magongo: everyone sat on low benches.

Fig. 27. Chairs were brought from the school to the church for us to sit on.

between the benches. The same pastor looked after both churches. This time he was taking no chances about people giving their money. He took the collection after the first hymn! And then at the end of the service he announced that some people had arrived after the collection was taken and that they should come forward and give their offering while we sang a final hymn! Vicky and I laughed about it at the time, but it seemed he had learnt nothing from our first visit.

The next time we went to Lang'ata, a year after our first visit, Paul directed us to go a different way, but we got lost in the middle of nowhere. We turned around to retrace our steps and when we came to some houses Paul got out to ask the way. The man he asked turned out to be someone he had been at college with many years before! There were lots of hugs and greetings and laughter. Then we were pointed in the right direction and given a young man to come with us to show us the way. It was a good job that we had him with us or we would have got lost again later. When we got to Lang'ata itself we again took a wrong turning. When we realised what had happened, Jim tried to turn the Land Rover round, but couldn't because a front spring had broken. So we were stranded! Two of our group stayed with Jim, while the rest of us walked through the village to the church. Paul asked the pastor to arrange for someone to go and help Jim, which he did.

I thought God must be going to do some amazing things, because certainly someone was trying to stop us getting there. By the time we actually arrived we were an hour late, but still the church was empty. So we went along to the church office and sat and had some water to drink while the people were summoned and we actually started the service at about 11.45 am.

The service was fine. No problem with the collection this time! Paul was invited to introduce the guests (the Bible study group), which he did, and then Mercy (the lady who had demons cast out of her with great difficulty the year before) walked up the aisle to speak. She said that she and her husband had wanted a child but that over the previous 5 years she had had one miscarriage after another. Then after she was prayed for the year before, she had got pregnant and one month ago had had a baby daughter! She brought the baby up in her arms and gave her to Paul. He held her up so that everyone could see her and then prayed for Mercy and the baby, giving thanks to God for His wonderful gift of a child.

After that the students who had waited with Jim and the Land Rover turned up to say that the Land Rover had been fixed. Hooray! I preached on the story of Bartimaeus from Mark 10:46-52, and how even today people try to discourage us from going to Jesus with our needs. Then I said that, just as Jesus was passing Bartimaeus on the road out of Jericho, he was actually in church today and they could bring their needs to him.

About 20 people came forward asking for prayer. We prayed in pairs: I was praying with one of the nursing students.

The first lady we prayed for was called Neema.[68] She asked us to pray for her baby who had a fever and was unwell. We prayed for the child and then asked Neema how she felt. She said, "I want to give my life to Jesus!" So we explained how to do that. She confessed her sins, I pronounced forgiveness and then we asked Jesus to fill her with the Holy Spirit. We then prayed for a lady called Grace who was complaining of pains in her thighs and cut her off from whatever was causing her frequent illnesses, and then for a man called Peter with pains in his chest.

That left a young woman who was demonized. She said she'd been to a witchdoctor in 1991. What a time we had with her. Initially nothing happened at all when we commanded the demons to leave in Jesus' name. Then all of a sudden there was a very loud cough. It was almost like a shot from a gun and it made me jump back. Then there was another period of nothing happening, and then lots of burping and belching. I lost count of how many demons came out, but it was very hard work and we had to keep swapping around. Paul came twice to help, but eventually she was free. There was one other demonized lady who was deaf and had a huge tumour on the right side of her neck (looking at it I assumed she had an inoperable cancer). The demons came out of her with quite a lot of noise but afterwards she was radiant. She wanted us to give her a lift back to KCMC when we left so that she could go to see a doctor about the lump in her neck. I told Paul to tell her that there was no point in wasting her time going to KCMC, because the lump was inoperable and her only hope was if God did something. He didn't want to tell her that, so we compromised by saying she should wait a week and if the lump was still there go to KCMC then. Obviously she took no notice at all, because I found her at the hospital the following morning with the lump completely gone!

---

[68] Neema means "Grace" in Swahili.

When Jesus was teaching in the synagogue at Capernaum a man who had an evil spirit in him shouted out and disrupted what was going on. Jesus commanded the spirit to be quiet and to leave the man.[69] We were finding on our travels that it was the same. Whenever we preached about Jesus, demons tried to disrupt what was going on. We didn't need the gift of discernment; the cause of the disruption was evident to everybody. At the end of the service we told the pastor to tell his people the following week that they should bring any charms, bracelets, idols, etc. that they had at home to the church so that they could be burnt.

Four years later we went back to Lang'ata to find a completely different atmosphere. We took a fellow dermatologist and his wife from America with us this time together with the students. There were loads of children to greet us on our arrival and they clambered all over the Land Rover, inside and out (Figs. 28 & 29). We weren't allowed to choose the Bible readings for the service, but I asked Paul

Fig. 28. The children welcome us at Lang'ata.

---

[69] Mark 1:21-28; Luke 4:31-37.

Fig. 29. Jim with the children who had clambered inside the Land Rover at Lang'ata.

to read Mark 10:13-16[70] at the beginning of the service. That was the only thing I had been sure that God had said when I was preparing my sermon – to have the little children come up to be blessed. Paul introduced us all. I preached on Mark 1:40-42, the story of the healing of the man with leprosy. We had already had readings from 2 Kings 5, Ephesians 3:14-20, and Luke 9:1-6, and a song about Samson and Delilah! After

---

[70] People were bringing little children to Jesus to have him touch them, but the disciples rebuked them. When Jesus saw this, he was indignant. He said to them, "Let the little children come to me, and do not hinder them, for the kingdom of God belongs to such as these. I tell you the truth, anyone who will not receive the kingdom of God like a little child will never enter it." And he took the children in his arms, placed his hands on them and blessed them.

the sermon I called out all the mums with small children and all the children for Jesus to bless them – loads. Then, all those who were sick – again masses of people. One lady we prayed for wanted to become a Christian and two ladies were demonised. There was a lot of power around. Paul said he had to cut his prayers short to stop people falling down. It all took until 4 pm. Then lunch! Then to Grace's house where more people were waiting for prayer.[71] Grace's son, Gabriel, had recently had a baby, so another cause for celebration. We didn't get home until 9.15 pm.

Three months later Paul came round one afternoon to report that Grace from Lang'ata had brought another demonised woman to his house the day before. He had prayed for her with Goodluck[72]. Apparently afterwards she was radiant and said to them that they would not be able to imagine how happy she was (she was Muslim, married but separated from a Christian man) and that she wanted to give her life to Christ.

A month after that Paul brought 2 sisters from Lang'ata to the Bible study group. They were called Hamida and Jaheleni, both Muslim names. When we asked them if they were Muslims, the answer was "Yes." Apparently Hamida had been sick for a long time. When we prayed, demons manifested and it took us about 50 minutes to get them all out. Paul then led Hamida in a prayer of repentance and acceptance of Jesus as her Saviour. She then looked very happy (Fig. 30). A few days later I went with Paul to see Mercy, the demonised lady that we prayed for at Lang'ata

Fig. 30. Hamida at the Bible study group after she had been set free.

---

[71] This is the Grace whose story is told at the beginning of this chapter.

[72] His neighbour who was a Pentecostal pastor.

Fig. 31. Mercy and her 3-year old daughter Joyce, who had been conceived after her mother was set free from demons at Lang'ata.

the first time we went there, and who had kept miscarrying. Her husband was now a pastor on the outskirts of Moshi, and we were able to see the 3-year-old daughter, Joyce, who had been conceived after Mercy was set free (Fig. 31).

When we first started going out on Sundays to village churches we went about once a month, but we ended up going somewhere every other week. Wherever we went, and whenever we went, we saw people become Christians, get healed, delivered and reconciled. If we preached about healing, people got saved! When we preached about salvation, people got healed! On one occasion I wrote in my diary when I got home, "I am so grateful to God for what He has done today in bringing forgiveness and healing and release. Certainly today has taught us as never before that we can do nothing ourselves. The only way anything happens is if Jesus does it."

CHAPTER 12

TEACHING OTHERS TO PRAY
FOR THE SICK

*After this the Lord appointed seventy-two others, and
sent them two by two ahead of him to every town
and place where he was about to go.*

Luke 10:1 NIV

In the autumn of 1994 Paul was invited to go to the Haggai
Institute in Singapore on an Advanced Leadership Course for
pastors from the third world. He was very excited about it
and told us that he had to raise £500 as a contribution to the
expenses involved in such a trip. I couldn't imagine where he
would find £500 from as his salary as a pastor was only about
£10/week. As I was praying one morning I thought that God
was telling me to give him the £500. I argued with God.
Where was I going to find £500? But God was persistent and
I felt compelled to tell Paul that we would pay for his trip to
Singapore. So he went. Interestingly, two weeks after I said
we would pay for his trip, I received some royalties from a
new book I had written just before I arrived in Tanzania. The
royalties more than covered the money we had given away!

Paul had a marvellous time in Singapore, prayed for many
sick people and made many new friends. He said that he talked
about our Bible study group everywhere and now people all over
the third world were praying for us. One of his new friends was
the pastor of a church in the Mathare slums of Nairobi (Fig. 32).
He had invited Paul to bring the group to his church to run a
weekend course on "Learning to pray for the sick."

The following March, five of us set off for Nairobi, having
been commissioned and sent out from St. Margaret's Church

Fig. 32. Mathare slums of Nairobi.

by its new pastor the previous Sunday. In the week leading up to the trip all five of us were ill. In the end I told Satan that if he thought he could stop us going to Nairobi by making us sick he was mistaken. Then I asked the Father to send the Holy Spirit to bring healing and peace. Within half an hour Jim was completely OK after three days of migraine. He ate some bread and jam and drank a cup of coffee, his first food in three days. The rest of us also got better before the weekend.

We drove to Nairobi on the Friday and started teaching at St. Christopher's Church, Mathare, on the Saturday morning. Paul taught on the Biblical basis for healing and then I did a practical session on "How to pray for the sick." Paul, Clara and Vicky demonstrated how to do it on a lady called Grace. God was very gracious in illustrating all I had been saying – giving a word of knowledge to Vicky, and manifestations of the Holy Spirit on Grace – eyelids fluttering, lips quivering and then tears. Then Paul prayed with authority and it was done. Grace said at the end, "I think God called this seminar just for me!"

We then had time for some questions before being taken to the home of one of the churchwardens for lunch. We got to see what Mathare was like as we walked through narrow alleyways full of water and rubbish and lots of people (Fig. 33). In the afternoon we taught about "The Kingdom of God" and "The use of Spiritual gifts in healing the sick," followed by another practical session.

On the Sunday I preached at the English service at 9 am. After the sermon twelve people wanted to become Christians and many more wanted healing. As soon as that service finished, the church filled up with more than three hundred people for the Swahili service. Paul preached at that service on lifting Jesus up like Moses lifted up the bronze snake in the desert.[73] He was very free and walked up and down the aisle with lots of actions and really got everyone involved (Fig. 34). When he finished he invited people forward for prayer. About a hundred people came forward – five to become Christians and the rest needing healing. Before the service Vicky had had a word of knowledge about

Fig. 33. Mathare slums: walking to the churchwarden's house for lunch.

Fig. 34. Paul Mtowe preaching at St. Christopher's Church, Mathare.

---

[73] Numbers 21:4-9; John 3:14.

someone called Peter. Amazingly there was only one man in the church called Peter – an old man walking with sticks, who was already on his way forward when Paul called out the name. It was really good to see God at work and I guess it was those two services more than the teaching on the day before that God had taken us to Nairobi for.

We were invited back to that church eighteen months later, this time to run an Alpha Course[74] for a week. This time only Paul and Clara and Jim and I were able to go, so we took The Kingdom Band[75] with us to help lead the worship. We all piled into the Land Rover plus all the instruments. Amazingly everyone and everything fitted in apart from two large speakers, which had to be tied onto the roof rack. We had a problem at the Tanzanian border because Jim's work permit had run out a month earlier. He thought he would be able to travel as my dependent, but the customs man at the border told him that he would have to pay $300 for a temporary permit to cover a week in Nairobi (or he could pay $100 unofficially!). The next thing I heard was that one of the band members had spoken to the customs official explaining the situation and that we didn't have to pay after all.

Interestingly not long before we went to Nairobi, Paul had been asked to go to see the high court judge in Moshi. The judge wanted the blessing of the local clergy. Paul told him if he judged on God's behalf, God would bless him, but if he judged for his own gain God would not bless him!

We also ran the Alpha course in the Bible study group, for the Swahili congregation at St. Margaret's Church, and as a way of training up young leaders in a secondary school on the outskirts of Moshi that was run by Ada and Godwin. For the English congregation at St. Margaret's we ran the "Saints for Healing" course.

---

[74] The Alpha course is an evangelistic course, which introduces the basics of the Christian faith through a series of talks and discussions.

[75] The Kingdom Band was a Christian band set up by one of Paul's sons with 4 of his friends – 3 guitarists, a keyboard player and a singer.

We were able to run training courses on "Learning to pray for the sick" in several churches in Moshi, at a new Bible School in Masama, and in the Cathedral in Arusha. The first time was in a Pentecostal church in downtown Moshi. Jim heard from one of the secretaries at work that it had been advertised on the local radio! It was touch and go whether it would be able to take place because there were very heavy rains for two of the three days it was on. There was a lot of flooding and the drive there and back was hairy to say the least. The Land Rover got stuck in a ditch at one point. The first night I went home in Paul's wellington boots by mistake. I didn't notice until I was walking home from the hospital the next day, when they seemed a bit big. It turned out that, in the dark the previous night, I put on Paul's boots by mistake. When he came to go home he found only my boots and they were too small for him. He had no other shoes with him, so someone had to piggyback him home!

As usual we taught the theory and then demonstrated how to pray. The first time we did it I got Paul and Vicky to pray for a lady. It turned out she was demonised – but they demonstrated very nicely how to pray and she shook and trembled and cried and smirked in triumph and then the demon was cast out. We then got the rest of the sick people out to the front and got 2 or 3 people to pray for each. It then seemed as if no one had learnt anything. They all had their eyes shut; they were praying aloud in tongues all together; some of the pray-ers were crying out in anguish. It was all pretty chaotic. There was a young girl who was deaf and dumb, who had been to a witch doctor and there was a young man who wasn't sick but who came out to give his life to Christ. Another old lady had tachycardia and pains in her leg and a man who was praying with her with two ladies was calling out, "Toka! Toka!"[76] over and over again. There were no signs of demons and when I asked him why he was saying, "Toka," he said that the last time he prayed with someone whose heart was beating very fast they had demons in them!

---

[76] Toka means "Get out" in Swahili.

Each day we taught, demonstrated, and then got them to have a go. By the end the atmosphere was completely different. There was no more shouting and behaving in bizarre ways. We also got those who had been prayed for the day before to come and say what had happened to them. The demonised lady that Paul and Vicky prayed for on the first day said that she had never able to go to sleep at night, and that the night after she was prayed for, she slept all through the night. It was a good three days, but not really long enough.

At an Anglican church in Majengo, near to where Paul lived, we quite often preached and led services. On one occasion at the end of the service there was a young woman who looked absolutely terrified. She asked for prayer and when we prayed for her it turned out that she was demonised. The demons kept manifesting but refused to leave. We sent for her husband and prayed for them in private after the service. She was called Venerita, and she was in church with her husband and baby daughter. It turned out that she had been perfectly well until the year before when her sister had died suddenly. The night that her sister died Venerita began to behave oddly. After a struggle the demons came out with a great deal of retching and coughing. Paul and I then went to her home (Fig. 35), anointed the doorpost (Fig. 36), and gave them a bottle of oil to do the same at her parents' house. She lived in a mud hut – one room – with her husband and baby. Following that Sunday morning the pastor of that church, Rogers Kitui, asked us to run a course and teach them how to pray for the sick themselves. He said he would be the first student!

Later we were asked to go to a new Bible school that was opening up at Masama. It was only 13 miles from Moshi, but it was a difficult cross-country journey, especially on the first day when it was pouring with rain. On the first day we just taught them how to pray for the sick, demonstrated how to do it and got them to have a go. And just like at the Pentecostal church in Moshi, they took no notice of anything we had said, and prayed just like they'd always prayed: all of them had their eyes shut and prayed long prayers. At lunchtime we had

Fig. 35. Venerita with her husband and daughter outside their house.

Fig. 36. Venerita's house. Paul Mtowe anointing
the doorpost.

a break where we were given bread and marge and peanuts; then back to work. On the second day, Goodluck offered to drive us there in his pickup truck (Fig. 37). The only problem was, we were all set to go but Goodluck couldn't be found. He had apparently gone to the garage to get his exhaust fixed. When he did turn up, he told us that we had to go back to the garage to fill up with petrol and to change one of the tyres which was completely bald and had a split in it. He'd been driving it like that, but we thought it was better to be late and get it fixed than find ourselves stranded miles from anywhere. We took the Kingdom Band with us to lead the worship. They were able to run their equipment off of Goodluck's car battery (Figs. 38-40), which worked really well (Fig. 41). We taught them about the Holy Spirit and prayed for them all to be filled with the Holy Spirit. In the late afternoon we had the dedication of the Bible School. Everyone marched around the outside of the building praying for God's blessing and protection over it, and then stood outside singing and praying together (Figs. 42 & 43).

Fig. 37. Piling into Goodluck's truck to go to the new Bible school at Masama.

Fig. 38. Connecting up the PA equipment to the car battery.

Fig. 39. Connecting up the PA equipment to the car battery.

Fig. 40. The PA equipment connected up to the car battery.

Fig. 41. The Kingdom Band.

Fig. 42. Masama Bible School: walking round the building praying for God's blessing on it.

Fig. 43. Praying for the new Bible School at Masama.

CHAPTER 13
NOT EVERYONE IS HEALED

For everything there is a season,
a time for every activity under heaven.
A time to be born and a time to die.
Ecclesiastes 3:1-2 NIV

We prayed for a number of people with cancer and AIDS; some were healed and some were not. One Sunday, when we went to Mwanga to take the service, we were asked if we would visit a lady called Michaelina who lived there. She had breast cancer, which had spread to her lungs and liver. We went to her house on the way to the church only to find that she had been admitted to KCMC that morning, so we ended up visiting her at the hospital on our way home. She had been admitted to hospital with pain in her belly from her huge liver, but she also had difficulty in breathing due to pleural effusions and ascites.[77] She seemed very pleased to see us and we prayed with her briefly.

Ten days later I went with Paul to visit her at home. We went on the bus, which took an hour and cost us £1 each. At a major road junction on the way Paul bought a bar of Imperial Leather soap through the bus window from a street vendor. When we got to the house, her husband and a number of other relatives welcomed us with open arms. They offered us a drink and asked us if we would prefer tea or a soda. I thought that tea would be the cheaper option, so I asked for that. More than an hour later it arrived! I hadn't realised that

---

[77] Pleural effusions are fluid in the pleural cavities around the lungs. Ascites is fluid in the abdomen.

they had no electricity, so someone would have had to light a wood fire to boil the water in order to make the tea.

It was only after we had drunk our tea that we were allowed to go into the bedroom to see Michaelina. I was instructed to talk to her and Paul would translate. I talked to her about knowing God for herself and that she could come to Him like a small child and tell Him what she wanted. She was interested in what I had to say but didn't really respond. Paul then prayed with her and anointed her with oil. When he was praying there was a real breakthrough and she was set free from many things from her past. There were lots of tears. Paul then got her husband and son to come and kneel by the bed and hold her hand and he prayed with his arms around both of the men. A lot of healing and reconciliation took place as they forgave one another for actions from the past. At the end of it Paul almost collapsed and he had to sit down. He said that strength had gone out of him. Afterwards Michaelina's face was radiant. Paul gave her the bar of Imperial Leather soap, which he'd bought at the bus stop, and I kissed her goodbye.

A month later, when the Bible study group went to Lang'ata on the Sunday, we stopped off at Mwanga on the way home, and went to see Michaelina at home. I didn't recognise her because she looked so well. She was up and about and her husband was very happy.

Three months later she was again in a bad way and was admitted to KCMC because of an accumulation of fluid in her belly. She had lost a lot of weight, was breathless, vomiting, and very tired. I visited her on the ward and I honestly thought that she was about to die. I asked her what she wanted Jesus to do for her, and she said, "Take me home!" I prayed with her then and went back later in the day to see how she was. Amazingly, after having the fluid in her belly drained off, she improved enough to go home. She lived for another two months. The day before she died she called for one of her sons, who had had a disagreement with his father, and told him to go and ask his dad's forgiveness, which he did. She then said that, since the family were now at peace, she was ready to die. Although obviously he was sad at her death, her husband was very much aware of God being there with them all the way through it.

At about the same time that we first met Michaelina, Paul came to the Bible study group one Thursday night very distressed because he had been praying for another lady in the hospital with terminal cancer. There was nothing that the doctors could do for her. Paul had been fasting and praying for her, but she had not improved. He had apparently promised her that the group would also pray for her. The next day I went to visit her on the ward. She told me that her husband visited her every day in the hospital, but that all he did was cry and ask her what was going to happen to him and their five children when she died. Who was going to take care of them? I asked her what she wanted Jesus to do for her. She replied, "Nothing really." She told me that she was a Christian and that in the five months that she had been ill, she had known God in a way that she had never known before. That she was so aware of how much He loved her and that He was closer to her than her husband and children. All she really wanted now was to go and be with Him forever. The next day I went to visit her again with Vicky and Goma. She was so pleased to see us. Vicky laid hands on her and prayed in tongues, and Goma prayed down the Holy Spirit on her, and then he kept saying, "Send more of your Holy Spirit, Lord! More power, Lord!" When we left she looked very, very happy. There was an amazing sense of it being done, whatever *it* was. The students and I continued to visit her and pray for her every day.

The following Thursday Paul brought her husband, Gilbert, to the Bible study group. We prayed for him asking God what He wanted to say to him. The gist of it was that he needed to hand his wife over to God; to release her, so that God could do what He wanted with her. We assured him that God loved her even more than he did and wanted what was best for her. That very day I had received a parcel of hankies from a friend in the UK. We used all of them that evening as Gilbert and others cried. His wife died two weeks later.

Soon after that we were asked to visit a lady at home in Moshi. When we got there we found a rather complicated family situation. The lady who was sick had apparently had four children and then, when her husband was away on business, had an extra-marital relationship and had become pregnant. When her husband found out he sent her back to her parents. Ten years later he decided he'd better take her back in order to take care of the children. He did so and took care of her but had no further sexual relations with her. Meanwhile he had five other wives and 19 children! He told us that his wife had stomach cancer, which had spread to her liver and lymph nodes. She had not been told what was wrong with her and was convinced that she was bewitched.

When we went into her bedroom we saw a lady who was just about skin and bone. The first thing she said to us was, "I'm dying!" Paul explained the gospel to her and talked about being forgiven and forgiving those who had hurt her. Then he prayed for her. She confessed her sins and forgave those who'd hurt her, but she was still in agony from the pain in her stomach. So I then went and laid hands on her and prayed in English, which Paul translated into Swahili. Real peace came upon her and after about two hours we sensed that what we'd come to do was done. It was such a privilege to be there!

One Sunday afternoon we were asked to go and visit a young man in a village half way up Mount Kilimanjaro. At 3.30 pm Jim drove me, Paul and his wife, Clara, and Vicky to the house. When we got there we found a young man with a painful swollen face and a large ulcer inside his mouth. I explained to him and his family that we had come to pray for him. Paul explained the gospel and led him to receive Christ as his personal Saviour. Then we prayed for him. He cried a lot and at the end said that he felt really well. When we finished praying we sang some songs of praise and he cried some more. Then we had to be given Coca Colas. By the time we got back home it was 8.30 pm and the electricity was off. Jim was not amused. I reminded him that some years earlier he had applied to an African missionary society. When they asked him what he could do, he said he could drive Land Rovers. They said that wasn't enough for him to be one of their missionaries and turned him down. I reminded him that now he was in Tanzania, God had allowed him to drive the team all over the country, and even into neighbouring countries in his Land Rover. Either we were there to do God's bidding or we weren't. Two weeks later we heard that the young man had died, probably of AIDS. The family were obviously upset, but delighted that he had been saved before he died. Apparently a local prayer group had been praying for his healing, but no one had thought to ask him if he knew Jesus or if he needed to be forgiven.

In those days Tanzania had no anti-retroviral drugs, so a diagnosis of AIDS was tantamount to a death sentence. Patients reacted in many different ways to hearing the diagnosis. One young man, who was an inpatient, immediately asked if he could go home to fetch his wife so that she could be tested too. He had only been married for 6 months. He said that if his wife was negative, he would send her home to her parents so that she wouldn't get infected. If she was positive, they would go back home together. Actually that was a remarkably refreshing attitude, very different to another young man who was in the ward at the same time who said that he wouldn't tell his wife that he was HIV positive, but that he would use a condom in future. Many patients on hearing the diagnosis asked for prayer. One man stood up in the clinic, lifted his hands up to heaven and prayed very loudly, asking Jesus to help him.

Several patients with AIDS came to the Bible study group asking for prayer. Paul had visited one young woman at home who had been unconscious and her parents thought that she was about to die. He had prayed for her and anointed her with oil, and within half an hour she had regained consciousness, got out of bed and danced around the room. A few weeks later she started coming to the Bible study group. She was still very thin, but looked absolutely radiant. She lived for another two years and in all that time she never stopped giving thanks to God for his goodness to her. Another lady in her fifties came regularly on a Thursday night. Her husband had died of AIDS, and she herself had lost weight, had thrush in her mouth, and acne on her face. We prayed for her every week. Three months later she said that she no longer thought of herself as being on the death list. She had put on 6 kg in weight, and both her thrush and her acne were better. She lived for two more years. Why did God heal her acne so that her skin looked normal, but not heal her AIDS? I don't know. She though was very happy to have got rid of her spots. One Thursday night she told us about a young Burundian refugee that she had met at the hospital. He had brought his son to KCMC for an operation. When the operation was delayed, the man had to return to the refugee camp in Burundi because his travel permit had run out. Back in Burundi he was arrested and put in prison for twenty days. There were so many prisoners in his cell that there was no room for anyone to sit or lie down. They all had to stand day and night. In desperation he suggested to his cellmates that they fast and pray for 24 hours. Usually ugali[78] was thrown through a small window into the cell once a day. At the end of the 24-hour fast, he found himself back in the house where he lived. He had no idea how he got there. The next day he heard that all the other prisoners in his cell had been executed. He travelled back to KCMC to collect his son who by now had had his operation. It was while he was at the hospital that he met the lady from the Bible study group. We had just been studying the story in Acts chapter 5 about the apostles being freed from prison by an angel. God was showing us yet again that He hasn't changed.

---

[78] Ugali is maize meal mixed with boiling water to the consistency of mashed potato and is the staple diet in Tanzania and the surrounding countries.

Several of our students did research projects related to AIDS. One lady from Namibia did a project on why African men don't use condoms. She had to give a talk about it at an international meeting a few months later. She was very nervous about having to speak in public and asked the Bible study group to pray for her. Afterwards she said that after prayer she was so changed that, like Jacob,[79] it was as if she had been given a new name. Certainly she spoke really well at the conference and having explained why men don't use condoms she said that God's standard was a man being married to one wife, and being faithful until one of them died. She said that this, and this alone, was the answer to AIDS.

One of the dermatology students, called Grace, became ill and was admitted to hospital. After two weeks of investigations she was found to be HIV positive. The doctor looking after her asked me if I would tell her. When I did so she cried a lot. I held her in my arms and she called out to God to help her. She told me that she had been a Christian since she was a child. She was married but separated from her husband who was an alcoholic; her sister was looking after her 7-year-old son. I talked to her about forgiving her husband and prayed with her about that. The very same day, Paul went to see her and did the same.

Since there was no treatment available for her she was discharged back to the student hostel. The other students told me that she must go home immediately. I told them that she wasn't yet ready to go home. They became very angry with me and told me that I didn't understand their African culture - that when you're sick you go home and let your family take care of you. I told them that we'd take things one day at a time, and I would arrange for her to go home when she wanted to go.

The day after she was discharged from hospital she asked me if I would take her to church with me on the following

---

[79] Genesis 32:22-28 (NIV).

Sunday. Jim and I picked her up in the Land Rover together with three other students and took her to St. Margaret's Church on the Sunday morning. Paul was leading the service and Godwin was preaching. Before the last hymn Paul called forward anyone who wanted prayer. Grace looked at me and asked if it was OK for her to go forward. I nodded, "Yes." Paul called several of us forward to pray with her. After a little while she showed signs of being demonised and collapsed, so Paul told the demons to go (quietly!) in the name of Jesus. He then anointed her with oil and told her to get up and walk, which she did. Afterwards she said she didn't understand what had happened; there had been a terrible darkness and then it went. The next day after work I went to see her in the hostel. She looked radiant and much less cachexic. She told me a miracle had happened the day before. She was full of joy. She told me that she hadn't been able to stop reading her Bible all day. She wanted to tell everybody about Jesus, and she said that she felt well physically. She had stopped all her pills, had eaten like a horse, and hadn't had any pain or vomiting. She had tried to tell some of the other students what had happened to her, but they had not been very interested. She had told Vicky on Sunday night what had happened, but she was the only one who had understood.

On the Sunday morning she had apparently felt unwell when she got up, but she said it was as if someone had told her "to go to church," so she felt that she had to. One of the other students was very cross with her and told her she should be resting on her bed, not going to church. But she just said she was going. She couldn't get over how good God had been to her and how wonderful He was.

I saw her every day for the next two weeks until she was ready to go home. In that time she came to terms with the fact that she was dying. One day she said to me, "You know, I used to be afraid of dying, but I'm not any more; in fact, I'm looking forward to it." One day when I prayed with her she saw a picture of herself walking up to a river with a large mountain on the other side. The river looked too deep to cross, but she managed to struggle across somehow. When she saw the steep mountain in front of her, she didn't think that she would be able to climb it. She looked up and saw a man in white robes at the top calling her forward, so she started up the hill. It was difficult, but when she got to the top He took her by the hand and said, "Come with me, my child." She wanted to look back the way she'd come, but He just said, "Come with me." A few days later she saw the same picture again, and this time God said to her, "Trust me!" She also told me that she was glad that God hadn't just healed her instantly, because then she might have said, "Thank you," but she might then have gone back to her old ways. She told me that she had come to know Him in a way that she previously hadn't thought possible, and how good He had been to her. When she talked about being ready to die, I asked her if it would be good to go home and see her son and she said it would. And so she was ready to go home and did so. She died a few days later.

A week after her death we had a memorial service for her in the RDTC hostel. Paul led it. Dr Grossmann had asked the students to choose one of their number from each year to speak about Grace at the service. The first-year students chose a friend of hers, Hilda, to speak. She spoke about Grace as a person - popular, active, friendly and very courageous at the end. The second-year students chose Faki, a devout Muslim man, to speak. I was absolutely furious with them. But when the time came for him to speak, he wasn't there. I silently gave thanks to God and the service moved on. Dr Grossmann spoke about Grace, her family and academic achievements. I spoke about what had happened to her in the last two weeks of her life – how she had met with God, knew her sins were forgiven and was looking forward to meeting Him face to face.

We sang several hymns and two separate groups of students sang – one in English and one in Swahili. Paul spoke on Ps.116:1-6: "*I love the Lord for he heard my voice; he heard my cry for mercy. Because he turned his ear to me, I will call on him as long as I live. The cords of death entangled me, the anguish of the grave came upon me; I was overcome by trouble and sorrow. Then I called on the name of the Lord. 'O Lord, save me.' The Lord is gracious and righteous, our God is full of compassion. The Lord protects the simple-hearted, when I was in great need, he saved me.*" It was very appropriate. He talked about death being the last enemy,[80] but that Jesus has overcome it: that they all needed to come into a relationship with Him and know that their sins were forgiven.

Just before the service finished, Faki walked in. He said he was sorry to be so late but he had fallen asleep. To my astonishment Paul invited him up to the front to say what he wanted to say about Grace. Oh, no! Faki said that everyone needed to be in a relationship with God and needed to be ready to meet Him. He said it was no good thinking there is plenty of time; there might not be. Grace was lucky in having people who talked to her at the end, so that her relationship with God was put right. Others might not be so lucky, so they should think about it now. I had been really cross with the students for choosing Faki to speak at Grace's memorial service, but God had His own plans[81] and good came out of it.

A week later I was able to reinforce what Faki had said when one of the first-year students told me that he couldn't do any work because he was too full of grief over Grace's death. I was able to talk to him about what had happened to Grace and how she had met with God in an amazing way in the last two weeks of her life. I told him that her dying was an opportunity for all of them to think about their own relationship with God and whether they too were ready to meet Him.

At one point it felt like almost everyone that we were praying for was completely beyond any kind of help. I remember saying to the students that our job was to pray for

---

[80] 1 Cor.15:26; 1 Cor.15:54-57 (NIV).
[81] Isaiah 55:8 (NIV).

the ones that God sends to us. It is up to Him what He does. Actually, it was wonderful to watch what God did for all those that we had the privilege to pray for and be alongside in their final days, weeks or months. I think all of them would, at the end, have echoed Paul's words from Philippians,[82] *"For to me, living means living for Christ, and dying is even better,"* as they looked forward to an eternity in His presence, and where there will be no more death or sorrow or crying or pain because these things are gone forever.[83]

---

[82] Philippians 1:21 (NLT).
[83] Revelation 21:3-4 (NIV).

CHAPTER 14
THE STUDENTS AT THE RDTC

*From Miletus Paul sent to Ephesus for the leaders of the
congregation. When they arrived, he said, "You know
that from day one of my arrival in Asia I was with you
totally - laying my life on the line, serving the Master no
matter what, putting up with no end of scheming by
Jews who wanted to do me in. I didn't skimp or trim in
any way. Every truth and encouragement that could
have made a difference to you, you got.*
Acts 20:17-20 The Message

The reason I had gone to Tanzania was to teach at the
Regional Dermatology Training Centre (RDTC) as well as
provide a dermatology service to patients with skin disease.
The students were great. They really wanted to learn and after
two years were fully equipped to do the work of a Dermatology
Officer in their local communities. For myself, because I was
able to teach the students every day for two years, instead of
just eight half days as I did in Southampton, there was a lot
more job satisfaction in terms of being able to see the progress
that was being made.

After the morning lecture the students were either assigned
to outpatients or the ward. If they were on outpatient duty
they would be the first person to see any patient. Once they
had done that they would then ask one of the consultants
to check what they had done. If the patient had something
that would be of interest to the whole group of students,
then the other students would be called to come and see the
patient too (Fig. 44). Every patient was a teaching opportunity.
As well as getting the diagnosis right, it was also important to

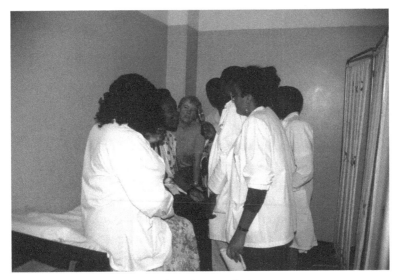

Fig. 44. KCMC: teaching the students in outpatients.

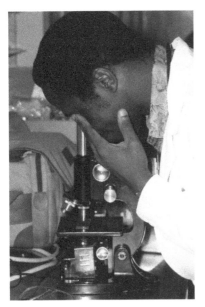

Fig. 45. KCMC: one of the students using the microscope in the skin clinic.

know what investigations were necessary and to get the treatment right. We had a microscope in the clinic so that skin scrapings could be examined for fungus on the spot (Fig. 45). Blood tests were done in the pathology department and biopsies on the ward.

The students were taught what treatments were available locally and how to make ointments themselves from the basic ingredients (Figs. 46 & 47). For example, whenever the tarmac roads were being repaired locally, I

Fig. 46. RDTC students learning to make ointments.

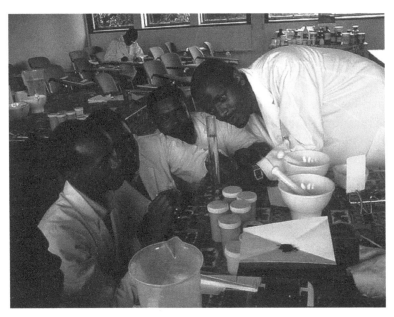

Fig. 47. RDTC students learning to make ointments.

Fig. 48. Tar from the road works in empty coffee tins.

would go with a few students and a couple of empty coffee tins, and ask for some tar (Fig. 48). It was always given to us free and we were able to mix it with Vaseline to make different concentrations of tar ointment to use for psoriasis. Even if the students came from a rural area, there would be a tarmac road somewhere within reach, which would need repairing at some time or other. It was no good them thinking that they would be able to use expensive drugs from America or Europe. They had to know what treatments would be available to them once they went back home and how to make them so that they were affordable to the patients.

If the students were assigned to the ward, then each day there would be a ward round, just as there would be in the UK (Figs. 49 & 50). Each day one student was on call for new admissions. Their job was to see the patient, take a history,

Fig. 49. KCMC. Ward round: getting out the patient's notes.

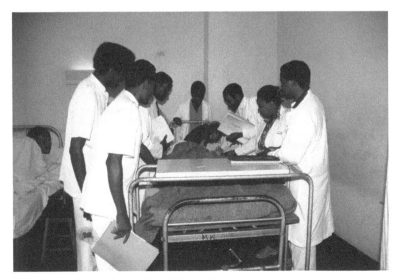

Fig. 50. KCMC. Ward round: bedside teaching.

examine him or her, make a diagnosis and a plan for how the patient was to be managed. The consultant would then be called to see the patient and go over the findings. A plan would be decided upon, and the student would then arrange for any investigations to be done and write the patient up for the treatment they needed. At the next ward round, that student would present the patient to the whole group of students and a discussion would follow and any corrective teaching put in place. We would see the patients on the male and female wards and then on the children's ward (Fig. 51), and then go and see any patients who were referred to us on other wards.

When the students first started, they had to learn how to do skin biopsies. Initially this was a group exercise, with everyone

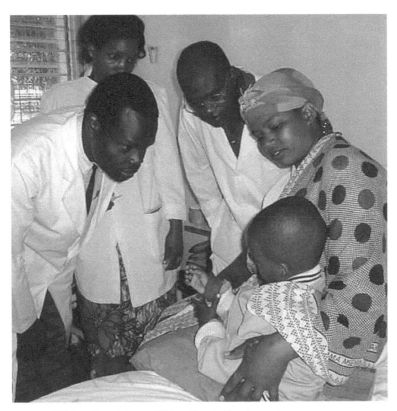

Fig. 51. KCMC. Examining a child on the children's ward.

helping (Figs. 52-55), but very quickly they were all proficient at doing them and could do them on their own. So if a skin biopsy was needed, then the student looking after that patient would do it. Soap was an expensive commodity. Carbolic soap came in bars approximately 15 inches long by 3 inches wide. This was then cut up into small bars for people to use. In between use it was locked away! Once the rubber gloves had been used they were washed and hung up to dry (Fig. 56)

Fig. 52. Learning to do a skin biopsy: putting on sterilised gloves.

before being sent to be sterilised. There was nothing that was disposable. All biopsies were sent to the pathology department

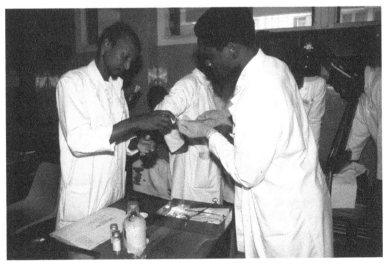

Fig. 53. Learning to do a skin biopsy: drawing up the local anaesthetic.

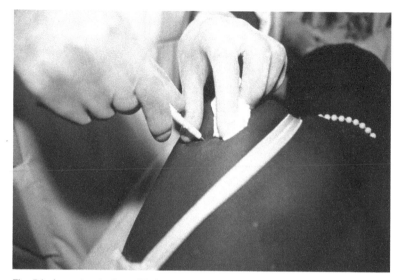

Fig. 54. Learning to do a skin biopsy: doing the actual biopsy.

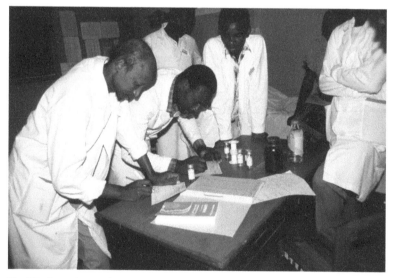

Fig. 55. Learning to do a skin biopsy: writing the pathology request form.

Fig. 56. Washed rubber gloves hanging up to dry.

where slides were prepared by the technicians for me to read. I spent a morning a week reading all the biopsies and writing a report on them. Anything really urgent could be rushed through and read in twenty-four hours. I picked out any slides of interest to use for teaching the students. We had an amazing projecting microscope, which projected the image onto a mirror on the ceiling, and then down onto a round table with a white top. That meant that the students and I could sit around the table and be up close and personal with the images. It was a good way to learn about the pathology of the skin in health and disease.

Lectures were held in the school of nursing (Figs. 57 & 58) and tutorials in the side room in the ward (Fig. 59). I got Pastor Mtowe to teach the ethics part of the course, which he and the students seemed to enjoy. The students had a special course on AIDS run by local nurses, where there was a lot of role play as well as formal teaching. The very first group of students also went to an AIDS conference in Nairobi for a week. I went with them and Jim drove us all in the Land

Fig. 57. The school of nursing.

Fig. 58. Early morning lecture to RDTC students in the school of nursing.

Fig. 59. Tutorial in the side room on the medical ward.

Rover. I had only been in Tanzania for six months and I had to organise for the students' registration and accommodation in another country. It was not at all easy as I wasn't able to get through on the telephone once. Fortunately we had some friends working in Kenya with MAF[84] and they organised it all for me. Twenty-four hours after we arrived the students all moved out of the accommodation that our friends had organised for them and found themselves something cheaper! Nevertheless the conference itself was good and we all learnt a lot. After that all the other groups of students got to participate in an AIDS conference somewhere in East Africa, and all went to Mwanza (on the shore of Lake Victoria) for field work in STDs[85] for two weeks.

At the end of each term the students had exams in the subjects that they had been learning about, and at the end of each year, exams in all six subjects that made up the advanced

[84] Missionary Aviation Fellowship.
[85] Sexually transmitted diseases.

diploma in dermato-venereology – general dermatology, sexually transmitted diseases, leprosy, pharmacology, primary health care, and teaching and learning methodology. At the end of the first year they had to devise a research project that they could carry out back home where they came from in the two-month break between the two years of study. Many of the students did projects on the prevalence of skin disease in their home area. This seemed like a good plan, as it would give them a good idea of the needs they would have to address at the end of the course. Some of the projects they did were:-

- Looking at how common skin diseases were in children under 5 years of age in a Maasai community.
- Looking at how health care workers in two regions of Tanzania treated scabies and ringworm in the community.
- Looking at the amount of disability in patients with leprosy in Kenya and Malawi.
- Looking at the prevalence of lymphatic filariasis on the island of Lamu in Kenya.
- Looking at the use of cosmetics and skin lightening agents among teenagers and adults in Nairobi.
- Looking at how many women attending antenatal clinics in a region of Tanzania had syphilis.
- Looking at how many patients attending STD clinics had already treated themselves before attending the clinic and why.

One year, three students, from Botswana, Namibia and Tanzania, all looked at how much urban and rural health care workers knew about the use of common skin ointments. The results were the same in all three countries. No one knew anything! When they got back to the RDTC after completing their projects they had to analyse the results and write up their work as a mini thesis. Some of the work was so good that it was published in a medical journal, and many of the students

Fig. 60. RDTC student presenting his research project at the annual CME conference.

presented their work at the CME[86] conference, which took place every January (Fig. 60).

I had gone out to Tanzania with the idea of being there for two years, which would have seen the first group of students complete their course. I loved being there. I loved the work. But I very quickly discovered that things happen much more slowly in Africa than they do in the UK, and that if I was to have any lasting impact I would need to write a textbook for the students. I had given them all copies of the two books that I had already written, but they were very much written for GPs in the UK. So at the end of my first year in Moshi, I spoke to Dr Grossmann about the possibility of staying on longer than two years. He seemed genuinely delighted so I then wrote to the University of Southampton to see what they would say. They gave me permission to stay for one extra year, but when I then wanted to stay longer they asked me to resign.

---

[86] Continuing Medical Education.

At about that time, one of Paul Mtowe's neighbours was talking about Tanzanian children being afraid of wazungu.[87] I said I'd have to get some boot polish then. But Paul said I didn't need to because my heart was the right colour! As I thought about it I realised that he was right. My heart was definitely in Tanzania and I felt more at home with the Tanzanians than with the foreigners (on the whole). Also his comment made me feel as though I belonged. It had been such an amazing experience working alongside people who accepted me unconditionally. I wrote in my diary that night, "I've been thinking today what a difference it makes to work alongside people who accept you unconditionally without criticism – how good it has been – and how good God has been to us as a result. Certainly He has been absolutely amazing these last few weeks and I believe it is one of the ways that He is encouraging me to trust Him for our future here. I have no doubts in my own mind that I will resign from Southampton and stay on here." And that is what I did. I resigned from my job in Southampton and committed my future to the RDTC.

The first year of the students' studies came to an end in July 1993 and they returned in September, together with twelve new first year students. We now had 26 students but only the same number of staff. How would we manage? The new second year students were given a lot more responsibility in the clinic and on the ward and we managed somehow. At one point a Christian nurse who I had known in England came to visit for a week and joined me in all that I did that week. When she left she gave me some money to buy a Swahili/English New Testament for each student. I was surprised to find that even the Muslim students wanted to have one! I wrote something in the front of each as I gave them out to the students and they passed them around among themselves eager to see what I had written.

---

[87] Foreigners (plural). Tanzanian children were afraid of foreigners because the ones they had met were mostly doctors who gave them injections.

Fig. 61. Wedding of a Zambian second year RDTC student at St. Margaret's Church. Paul Mtowe conducting the service.

A month before the first group of students were going to sit their final exams one of the students announced that he wanted to get married! After counselling the couple, Pastor Mtowe conducted the service at St Margaret's Church (Fig. 61) and all the students and staff were there to witness it. The female students all made outfits from the same cotton material but in different styles (Fig. 62), which is an African custom.

Four weeks later came the final exams. The written papers had to be hand written and taken to Dar-es-Salaam for approval by the University and typed up and printed by them so that there was no chance of cheating. Unfortunately we had no control over what came back to us. On the first occasion when I broke open the seal on the envelope for the first paper, I found a pharmacology question in the middle of the general dermatology paper. I made the decision to tell the students to cross out that question and answer the others. Fortunately there were no adverse repercussions from my actions. We also had to have an external examiner approved by the University.

Fig. 62. Female students from the RDTC all dressed in outfits made from the same material for the wedding.

On two occasions the external examiner, who they had approved, let us down by deciding not to come at the last minute! Of course they hadn't let us know they weren't coming. It was an absolute nightmare. The first time, it just so happened that an American dermatologist, who was coming to spend six months with us, arrived the night before the exams started. But how could we get permission for him to be our external examiner? My Tanzanian colleague stayed up all night trying to get through to someone in Dar-es-Salaam on the telephone who had the authority to give us permission. We finally got it at 6 am on the morning the exams started!

When the exams were over, the students who had completed the first year of their studies were put in charge of the clinic and the ward and we took the second-year students on a camping trip to Ngorongoro Crater for a weekend. When we arrived at the campsite we found two male elephants fighting just where we were going to pitch our tents (Figs. 63 & 64). After supper we sat around a campfire telling stories (Fig. 65). The students were so scared about animals coming in the night

Fig. 63. Elephant on our campsite on the rim of Ngorongoro Crater.

Fig. 64. The students' campsite on the rim of Ngorongoro Crater.

Fig. 65. RDTC students and Henning sitting round the campfire after supper.

that nearly all of them sat around the campfire all night and didn't go to bed. The next morning we drove down into Ngorongoro Crater to see the animals (Fig. 66). We saw lots of lions, and at one point when we stopped to watch them the lions decided to lie down under our Land Rover. It was the only place of shade. When we wanted to move on they were reluctant to move (Fig. 67). As well as watching the animals, the students all had their photos taken with a group of Maasai warriors (Fig. 68). For a fee of course!

When we got back to Moshi we had an informal graduation service and dinner for the graduates. Three of the fourteen students in that first intake of students got more than 80% in all six subjects and were awarded a distinction by us and the University (Fig. 69). Jim designed and printed some certificates for them to take home (Fig. 70) because the official graduation took place in Dar-es-Salaam six months later (Fig. 71). Only the students from Tanzania and Kenya were able afford to come back for that. The rest received their official diplomas by post.

Fig. 66. Driving down into Ngorongoro Crater.

Fig. 67. Lions under one of our Land Rovers in Ngorongoro Crater.

Fig. 68. Three RDTC students having their photo taken with some Maasai men.

Fig. 69. The 3 RDTC students who got a distinction in all 6 subjects in their final exams: one from Kenya, one from Uganda and one from Tanzania.

Fig. 70. Second group of RDTC graduates. Informal graduation ceremony at KCMC immediately after the exams.

Fig. 71. Official graduation ceremony at the University of Dar-es-Salaam.

Fig. 72. KCMC. RDTC student hostel with the red roof (centre); nurses hostel (left); Hospital (right).

For the students who had been part of the Bible study group, we also gave them a certificate to say that they had completed a one-year training course on praying for the sick and ministering in the power of the Holy Spirit. Paul and I both signed it and we gave the certificates out during a communion meal together just before they went home.

During the second year I was there the student hostel was built, and our students at last had their own home (Fig. 72). Two students shared a study bedroom and there was a large sitting room and kitchen where they could cook (Fig. 73). In January 1997 the purpose-built dermatology unit was finished (Fig. 74) and opened by the Prime Minister (Fig. 75). One of our students met him as he arrived and welcomed him to the RDTC (Fig. 76). We were going to hire a red carpet for him to walk on but the cost was prohibitive. One of the nurses had the idea that we could scatter bougainvillea petals instead, which produced a much more pleasing effect (Fig. 77).

After that our lives were transformed. We really could practice proper medicine now! We had lots of clinic rooms

Fig. 73. RDTC student hostel: the kitchen.

Fig. 74. RDTC: our new purpose built building.

Fig. 75. Official opening of the new RDTC building.

Fig. 76. One of our students welcoming the Prime Minister of Tanzania.

Fig. 77. Official opening of the RDTC building: red carpet made of bougainvillea petals.

where the patients could be seen in private (Fig. 78). We had two operating theatres, a laboratory, a room with a decent microscope where I could teach pathology and take photos of the slides, our own pharmacy, a library, a lecture theatre and several smaller teaching rooms (Fig. 79). In addition we had offices where we could work when we were not in the clinic or on the ward. When I eventually returned to Southampton, I missed the facilities at the RDTC, and the freedom to do your absolute utmost for each patient without red tape and health and safety issues getting in the way.

Every day I lectured to the students either in the morning or in the afternoon or both. It was pretty informal with questions at any time. I would often wander up and down as I was talking, and one morning I noticed that a student in the front row had unusual fingernails. When I looked at them more closely I found that they were blue in colour. I knew that this young man had recently been in hospital with malaria and I assumed that the blue colour of his nails was due to the

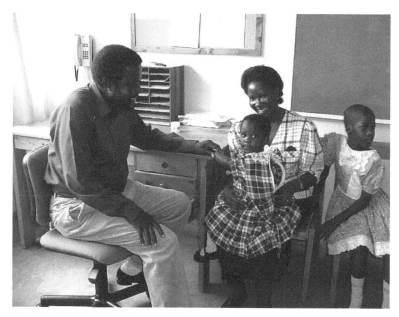

Fig. 78. RDTC building: Dr John Masenga seeing a patient in one of the new clinic rooms.

Fig. 79. RDTC building: Dr Henning Grossmann teaching in one of the smaller teaching rooms.

chloroquine[88] that he had taken. I took some photos of his nails, with his permission, and thought nothing more of it, until I heard that nine months after he had completed his course, he had died of AIDS. That made me wonder if I was mistaken about the cause of his blue nails. I devised a questionnaire to ask patients how many times they had had malaria in the previous three months and in the previous twelve months, and how many courses of chloroquine they had taken in the previous three and twelve months. The students administered the questionnaire to all medical inpatients on a single day, and repeated it a month later. On each occasion they also looked at the patient's finger and toenails to see if they were blue or not, and checked in the patient's notes to see if they had been tested for HIV infection. We found seventy-five patients with blue nails, but there was no difference in the number of episodes of malaria or the number of occasions when they had taken chloroquine, in patients with or without blue nails. But, every single patient with blue nails tested positive for HIV infection. This proved to be a very useful sign to look for, and one that anybody could notice. Many students wrote to me after they had finished their studies and had gone home, to say that they were finding blue nails a very useful marker of HIV infection. It isn't quite so useful any more since anti-retroviral agents are now widely available in Africa, and AZT[89] is also known to cause blue nails. At the time of our investigation AZT was not available in Tanzania and none of our patients was taking it. Trying to find the cause of blue nails was a very practical example to the students of what you can achieve if you don't just give up when you see things you don't understand. Any one of them would be able to discover something new that

---

[88] At that time chloroquine was the most common treatment used for malaria.

[89] AZT is azidothymidine, also known as Zidovudine.

might be really helpful to their patients. They just needed to notice it, and then set about investigating it and proving it.

In exactly the same way they were able to take part in proving whether oral ivermectin[90] was a good treatment for scabies or not. In the summer of 1996 we had a number of men from the local prison escorted to the clinic for advice about their skin. They came handcuffed to a prison officer and all of them had scabies. There was no point in our treating the twenty men who came to the clinic without finding out how many other prisoners had scabies too. So I visited the prison and discussed the problem with the prison officer in charge of the prison and the two medical personnel working there – a medical assistant and a rural medical aide. It was obvious that scabies was widespread, but there would be a problem in treating it properly because the prison could not afford the treatment. The students and I had recently been looking at a paper in the New England Journal of Medicine where the American authors had treated twenty-two patients with scabies with oral ivermectin. Half of their patients were otherwise healthy and half were HIV positive. They reported that it worked well, so we thought that we might try it. At that time ivermectin was not licenced for treating scabies, so I wrote to Merck Sharpe and Dohme Interpharma, who made ivermectin, and who had been supplying the drug free of charge for the treatment of onchocerciasis in all endemic countries for more than a decade. They kindly donated enough tablets to treat all the prisoners.

Five further visits to the prison followed. On the first day, together with one of the dermatology graduates who was now working at the RDTC, I examined 1153 prisoners. They came cell by cell. Each man stripped off so we could examine his skin, weigh him, and depending on his weight give him a single dose of ivermectin. We watched each prisoner swallow

---

[90] Ivermectin is a drug that is used for all kinds of parasitic infections, particularly onchocerciasis (river blindness) in Tanzania.

the tablets with a cup of water. It took us all day and well into the evening to see all the prisoners. We ended up examining the last prisoners by torchlight! We then went back after one, four, eight and twelve weeks to see what had happened to the men. After just one week, many of the men waved at us as we drove up to the prison shouting out their thanks and saying that they were better.

After the first visit I realised it wasn't going to be practical for just two of us to keep examining 1153 patients in a day, so I enlisted the help of four Tanzanian[91] second year students to help. The drug worked really well. After eight weeks 95.5% were cured. Those who were not better were treated with the normal topical treatment and by the week twelve visit, scabies was no longer in evidence. We also examined all members of the prison staff and treated them and their families where necessary. When the treatment was over I wrote a report explaining the nature of scabies, how it is transmitted from person to person and how to prevent such an outbreak in future. I discussed the report with the officer in charge of the prison, the regional prison officer and the two medical personnel; they were each given a written copy, and copies were also sent to the Minister of Health, the principal commissioner of prisons, the director of medical services, prison division, and the regional medical officer for the Kilimanjaro region. It was a big learning experience for all of us, but showed what could be done if you were willing to try to find a solution to a problem.

There have now been two hundred and seventy two graduates from sixteen African countries (Fig. 80). 80% of them are training others as well as running skin and STD clinics. Several are in positions of authority in their own countries. For example, a Malawian graduate heads up the STD and leprosy services for the whole of Malawi, a Tanzanian graduate is Dean of a Clinical Officer Training School in

---

[91] I used Tanzanian students so that there was no language problem with speaking to the prisoners.

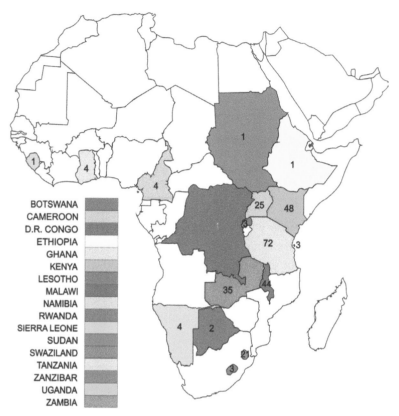

Fig. 80. Map to show where the RDTC graduates are from.

Northwest Tanzania, and another is on the staff of the RDTC, and is playing a leading role in setting up STD clinics for truck drivers along the routes taken through Tanzania. But the whole process was not just about education and being equipped to do a good job. At the graduation dinner they loved to dress up and look good (Figs. 81 & 82), but it wasn't just about looking good. On Maundy Thursday each year at the Bible study group, we washed each other's feet (Fig. 83). What I hoped for was that all the students who graduated from the RDTC would be prepared to go home and do their work in humble service for their patients.

Fig. 81. RDTC student from Lesotho dressed up for the graduation party.

Fig. 82. RDTC student from Tanzania dressed up for the graduation party.

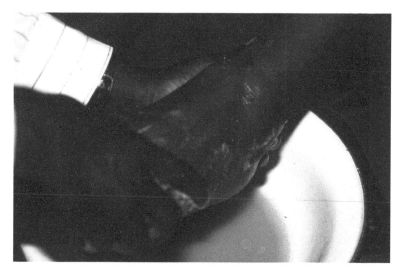

Fig. 83. Washing one another's feet.

CHAPTER 15
OTHER WORK AT THE RDTC

*Whatever you do, work at it with all your heart, as
working for the Lord, not for men.*
Colossians 3:23 NIV

Moshi is situated just below the equator and for most of the year
there are twelve hours of sunshine every day. This is very bad
news for the albinos who are living there, of whom there are a
large number.[92] Patients with albinism do not have the melanin
pigment in their skin which is there to protect you from the sun,
and as a result they develop skin cancers in their twenties and
thirties which may kill them. [93] When a baby is born in Moshi,
the mother and child stay in the house for the first three months
of the baby's life. The mother is fed a high protein diet and
mother and baby are taken good care of. After three months life
goes back to normal. The baby is strapped to mum's back as she
goes back out to work in the fields (Fig. 84). This means that
from the age of three months the face and scalp of all babies are
exposed to the sun for twelve hours a day. By the age of twelve
months, all albino babies have evidence of sun damage. Once
children go to school things are not much better, as many lessons
take place out of doors (Fig. 85).[94] Children with albinism also
have problems with their eyes. Most can only count fingers at

[92] The incidence of albinism in Tanzania was 1 in 1700 of the population.
In the UK it is 1 in 20,000.
[93] The youngest albino I saw with skin cancer was 16 years old. One died at
the age of 24.
[94] In a study we did we found that children spent between 2 and 5 hours out
of doors at school each day; this included doing lessons, gardening and
playing.

Fig. 84. Albino baby strapped to mother's back leaving his face and head exposed to the sun.

six metres, so they can't usually read what is on the blackboard. There was no provision in the schools for this poor vision other than allowing the children to sit at the front of the class. There were no magnifying glasses or large print books. If children do not get a good education it means their options for work when they leave school are severely limited. In practice this means that most will only be able to work in the fields (Fig. 86), leaving them exposed to the sun most of the day for the rest of their lives.

Fig. 85. Children at primary school doing their lessons out of doors.

Fig. 86. Albino lady working on the land.

Jim and I were welcomed with open arms when we arrived in Moshi, but the local albinos, with the same colour skin as us, were ostracised. People called them rude names and were unwilling to sit with them, eat with them, shake hands with them, employ them or marry them. Mainly this was because of the widespread belief that the condition is due to a curse or a punishment for some kind of misdeed by the mother, such as:-

- Evil spirits which come to create havoc in a family
- Spirits from Europe which come and invade Africans
- A child of the devil who snatches away the African child during delivery and replaces it with an albino
- The reincarnation of a murdered albino (until 60 years ago nearly all albino babies were smothered at birth because of the superstitions about this condition)
- Infidelity with a European
- Couples having intercourse when the woman has her period
- She didn't keep to the customary rules of diet while she was pregnant
- She ridiculed an albino or was cruel to one

Fig. 87. Albinos waiting for the albino clinic at the Health Centre at Keni. Most of them were sitting in the sun to keep warm!

Since I left Tanzania the horrible practice of killing albinos has happened, with more than eighty having been killed since 2001. This has apparently been so that their body parts can be used by witch doctors to bring good fortune to others. The government has brought in legislation to stop it, but many albinos still fear for their lives.

Soon after I arrived in Moshi I saw an albino man with some precancerous lesions on his skin. He told me that there were lots of albinos living in the rural areas around the base of Mount Kilimanjaro and he invited me to meet some of them. I agreed to go with him to a health centre about 50 km from Moshi.

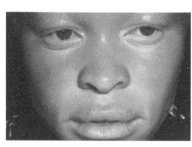

Fig. 88. Albino lady with sunburn.

When we arrived about fifteen albinos were waiting for us. Most of them were sitting out in the sun even though there was plenty of shade available (Fig. 87). All had severe sunburn (Fig. 88). They had no idea of the importance of protecting themselves from the sun, but even if they had known, there was nothing they could easily have done about it.

Don Lookingbill, a dermatologist from Pennsylvania, came to spend his six-month sabbatical at the RDTC, [95] and he also was concerned about how we might help the albinos. Together we set up ten clinics around the base of Mount Kilimanjaro, where the albinos could come for advice twice a year.

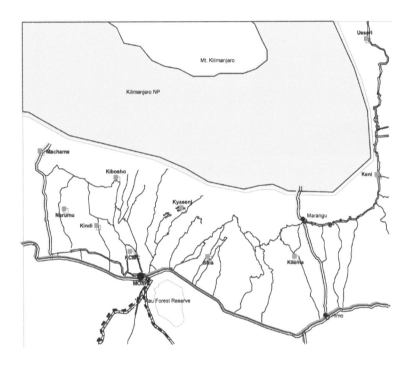

Map to show location of albino clinics

On the first Tuesday of every month we would set off in the RDTC Land Rover (Fig. 89), through the Tanzanian country-side (Fig. 90) to visit one, two or three dispensaries, health centres or small hospitals in villages (red squares on the map above) known to have a large number of albinos.

---

[95] July to December 1993.

Fig. 89. Don Lookingbill driving the RDTC Land Rover to an albino clinic.

Fig. 90. Route to the albino clinic at Shia: Mount Kilimanjaro in the background.

At the beginning all the albinos we saw were sunburnt (Fig. 91). All children had evidence of chronic sun damage by the age of 12 months.[96] Precancerous lesions appeared from about the age of eight and every albino had these by the age of thirty. Fifty per cent of

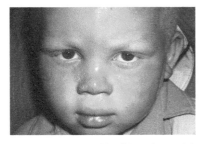

Fig. 91. 4-year old albino boy with sunburn.

albinos over the age of thirty had one or more skin cancers, some of which were very aggressive and resulted in the patient's death. The youngest patient with a skin cancer was only 16 years old.

Avoiding the sun completely was not an option in Tanzania, but we thought that getting the albinos to protect themselves from the sun might be possible. We decided that we would try. We provided broad brimmed hats, long sleeved shirts and blouses and a homemade topical sunscreen. None of these had previously been available.

We had the hats made in a local tourist shop. Beige was the only option for colour so that is what we had. The albinos wore them, but they didn't like them because they were the same colour as the hats worn by the army. They said that they would like blue hats, so we managed to get the second batch made in blue. These were much more popular but not very suitable for children under the age of two (Figs. 92 & 93), and they didn't survive being washed very well (Figs. 94 & 95). Later we bought pairs of second hand trousers in the local market and made the hats ourselves, lining them with old fertiliser bags to give a nice stiff brim (Fig. 96). These lasted much better than the tourist hats, and it gave us a choice of different colours and materials that individuals could choose

---

[96] The sort of wrinkling that you would expect to see in a 60 or 70-year-old in the UK.

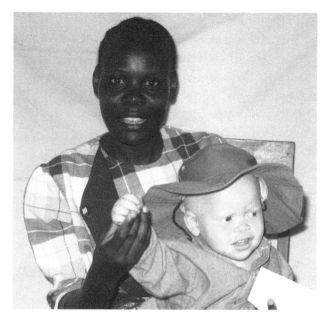

Fig. 92. Wide-brimmed hat to keep the sun off he face.

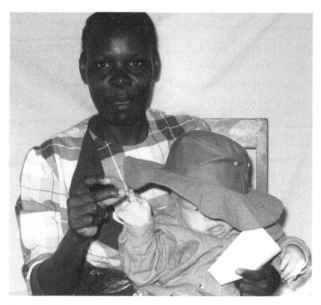

Fig. 93. Wide brimmed hat not very practical for a 15-month old child.

Fig. 94. The wide-brimmed albino hats did not survive well after washing.

Fig. 95. The wide-brimmed albino hats did not survive well after washing.

Fig. 96. New style wide-brimmed hats made from second hand trousers and fertiliser bags.

Fig. 97. Foreign legion-style hat.

from. Later still we made foreign legion style hats (Fig. 97) by sewing pieces of material onto the rim of second hand baseball caps. All of these hats protected the face, scalp, neck and ears, but the rest of the skin also needed protecting.

We advised wearing long sleeved shirts or blouses, long trousers or long skirts and shoes and socks. We had to get special permission for school children to wear long sleeved shirts or blouses because the school uniform was always short sleeved. Unfortunately long sleeved shirts and blouses were a lot more expensive than short sleeved ones and many parents couldn't afford them. To get around this problem we simply bought up large numbers of second hand cotton shirts and blouses, washed and ironed them and gave them out in the clinics (Fig. 98).

At that time there were no sunscreens available anywhere in Tanzania so we had to make our own from the raw ingredients sent out by an American dermatologist. Each month Don Lookingbill and I made up batches of sunscreen in our kitchens for the next clinic (Fig. 99). In the clinic we explained how to

Fig. 98. Second hand long-sleeved blouse being tried on in the clinic, assisted by one of the RDTC students.

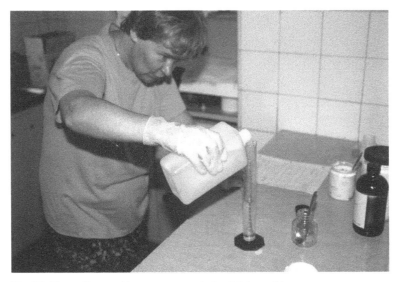

Fig. 99. The author making sunscreens in her kitchen at home.

Fig. 100. One of the RDTC students showing mum how to use the sunscreen on her child.

use the sunscreen, demonstrated how to use it (Fig. 100) and gave each albino enough to last for the six months until the next clinic.

Fig. 101. Explaining to mum all she needed to know about how to care for her albino son.

I got one of the students to help me write an educational booklet, which we could give to the parents of albino children (Fig. 101), adult albinos, the local health care workers, local school teachers and our students at the RDTC. The booklet (Fig. 102), available in either Swahili or English, explained what an albino was, how you became an albino, what difficulties you would face and how to protect yourself. Obviously we went through it with them in the clinic (Fig. 103).

We aimed to see all albino babies as soon as possible after they were born (Fig. 104). The local RMAs, MAs or AMOs were all spoken to and given a supply of the educational book-lets in Swahili to give to the parents of new born albino babies. Armed with the information themselves, they were then able to explain to the parents how to protect the child and book them in to the next albino clinic in the area. We wanted all albino children to start sun protection as early as possible. I was always delighted when children came to the clinic properly protected (Fig. 105).

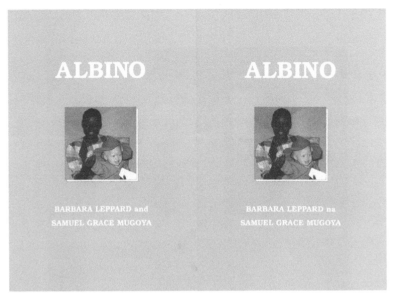

Fig. 102. Albino educational booklet available in English or Swahili.

Fig. 103. The author going through the booklet with an adult albino.

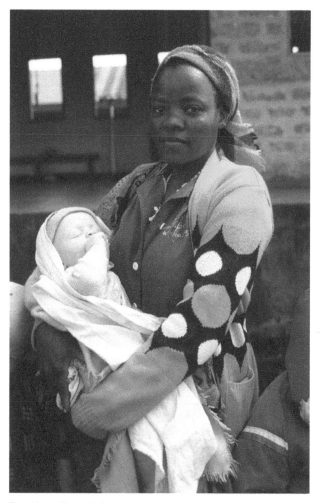

Fig. 104. Albino baby coming to his first appointment in the albino clinic.

Fig. 105. Albino boy nicely protected from the sun.

It was already too late to help the adult albinos as far as preventing skin cancer was concerned. Of course we saw adults as well as children in the clinics and gave them advice, hats and sunscreens and dealt with any lesions they had on their skin. In each village we appointed a local albino co-ordinator, usually a mother who was already taking good care of her albino child. Her job was to make sure the albinos all came to the clinic, and between clinics to make sure that the children were properly protected from the sun. Two weeks before each albino clinic, a message was sent to the local churches to tell them that we were coming. For two Sundays they would give out a message in the services to tell everyone when and where they should come to be seen. It was a system that worked pretty well.

Pat Montgomery, the dermatologist in Winchester,[97] sent me a gadget for transforming carbon dioxide gas into solid carbon dioxide with which I was able to treat the precancerous conditions that the albinos developed (Figs. 106-108). I bought two

Fig. 106. The author making solid carbon dioxide from the gas in the cylinder.

---

[97] My dermatological colleagues back in the UK were very supportive the whole time that I was in Tanzania.

carbon dioxide gas cylinders in Nairobi;[98] when the cylinders were empty we were able to refill them for free from the local Coca Cola Company in Moshi.

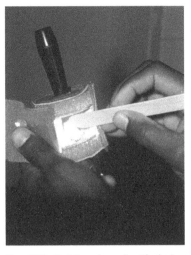

Fig. 107. Solid carbon dioxide being collected.

If albinos came to the clinic with skin cancers, we took them back to KCMC with us at the end of the day. When we got back, I took them to the ward, cut the cancers out in the side room, gave them a bed for the night and sent them home on the bus the next day. Later I took all the equipment that was needed to remove tumours to the clinics with me and operated there and then which saved everybody a lot of time.

Fig. 108. Solid carbon dioxide being used to treat a precancerous lesion on the back of an albino's hand.

I remember one clinic where a brother and sister both came to the clinic with a skin cancer. They told me that they had another albino sister at home. When I asked why she hadn't come with them to the clinic, they told me that she couldn't come because she had skin cancer. That didn't sound like a good excuse to me, especially since they had both come. We planned to take them both back to KCMC with us that afternoon, and when they told us that our journey back would practically take us

---

[98] I was able to buy them when Jim and I took the students to the AIDS conference in Nairobi.

past their house, I decided that we would stop off and see their sister. We parked the Land Rover by the side of the road at the nearest point to their house and set off across a field to see the sister. After half an hour I was getting a bit fed up because of the time it was taking. I kept asking them how much further it was to go? The answer was always the same. Not much further! After an hour I was beginning to get angry. But we eventually arrived at the house and the sister was brought out to see us. Her face was covered with a cloth. When it was removed I saw that more than half her face was eaten away with skin cancer and that her left eye was hanging out of the eye socket on a stalk. She was 32 years old. I felt so ashamed of myself that I had thought she should have come to the clinic and that I had moaned about walking for just over an hour to see her. Unfortunately there was nothing I could do for her: the cancer was too extensive. I did take her brother and sister back to the hospital and cut their more modest cancers off. While I was in Moshi twelve albinos died of inoperable skin cancers like hers.

Most cancers were on the face but one man had 37 tumours all over his body. I arranged with one of the surgeons to give him a general anaesthetic and between us to cut all the tumours off. We also saw two men with extensive cancers on the leg and foot. Both needed to have amputations, which were done at KCMC. After their operations they were provided with an artificial leg made at the school of orthopaedic technology. One man was so grateful for what had been done for him that he never failed to turn up at the clinic and always looked really cheerful (Fig. 109). The other man never appeared again. When he'd missed three clinic appointments (18 months) I went to visit him at home. I found him sitting outside his house perfectly well (Fig. 110). He didn't like wearing his artificial leg and preferred to get around using a crutch or just by hopping, which was why he hadn't been able to come to the clinic. We found his "new leg" hanging up on the wall inside his house!

Fig. 109. Albino man who had an amputation for a big tumour on his foot: he is coping very well with an artificial leg.

Fig. 110. Albino man sitting outside his house. He had had an amputation of his right leg for a very large tumour on his lower leg: his artificial leg was hanging up on the wall inside!

Right at the beginning of the albino project one man told me that they didn't want my do-goodery! He said he was fed up with foreigners saying that they had come to help, when it was always only temporary. What he actually said was, "You come out here for a year, give us medicine and then leave us with nothing." He had a good point. We therefore made sure that the albino clinics were integrated into the teaching programme of the RDTC, so that they could continue indefinitely. On each of our monthly visits we[99] took two students with us, to help with the clinic and to teach them how to run something similar, if they wanted to, when they got home.

When I left Tanzania I appointed a full time albino co-ordinator with the aid of a grant from the Italian Rotary Club. He would work with Alfred Naburi, one of our graduates who was working at the RDTC, to continue running the clinics and to increase the education programme that we had started. This would include teaching those at teacher training colleges as well as kindergarten, primary and secondary school teachers, and the general public through newspaper and magazine articles, and radio and television programmes. The ten albino clinics I set up are still running, and the RDTC graduates have set up new ones in other parts of Tanzania and in the neighbouring countries of Kenya, Malawi and Zambia. I was looking after four hundred albinos. The RDTC is now looking after fifteen hundred albinos.

It was always going to be a long-term project. I knew from the beginning that we would not know whether our strategy of protecting the children had worked for twenty years. Imagine my delight when I heard Henning Grossmann say

---

[99] All the dermatologists who came out to help at the RDTC for 6 months or a year helped with the albino clinics. I am grateful to all of them for their help, especially Don Lookingbill, Jim Nordlund, Sandy McBride, Rosemarie Moser, Lucius Gilli, Ben Naafs, Marv Weinreb and Lorne Albrecht.

Fig. 111. Collecting a donated sewing machine to give to an albino lady so that she could earn her living making clothes.

in 2013 that they had not seen a single serious cancer in the previous year.[100]

Most of the adults that we saw were concerned about getting work that they could do inside. Some of the ladies wanted to learn tailoring so with some donated sewing machines we tried to set that up (Figs. 111 & 112) with a local seamstress available to teach them. Unfortunately it didn't work. But in 2012 a "Care Unit for Persons with Albinism"[101] was built in the grounds of the RDTC (Fig. 113). Inside is a tailoring school, which is flourishing and enabling albino

---

[100] Exactly 20 years after we started.

[101] Financed by the International League of Dermatological Societies, the International Foundation for Dermatology, Under the Same Sun (a Canadian NGO) and Rotary International.

Fig. 112. Albino lady who has just received a donated sewing machine.

Fig. 113. New building for the care of albinos in the grounds of the RDTC.

Fig. 114. Tailoring school inside the building shown in Fig. 113.

women to earn a living by their sewing (Fig. 114). In the other half of the building is a unit making sunscreens with an SPF of 30+. A Spanish pharmacist, Mafaldo Soto Valdes, runs it and last year made 15,000 jars of sunscreen (Fig. 115). So all albinos can now be given sunscreens without me struggling to make enough bottles every month.

While working at the RDTC I had the chance to travel to the USA, England, Italy, Kenya and South Africa, to talk about what we were doing in Moshi. It caught most people's imagination, and I found it a great privilege to meet with dermatologists around the world who were supportive of what we were doing. I was able to do a drug trial for a Belgian drug company comparing two different antifungal agents for which they gave money to build two staff houses on the doctors' compound at KCMC. The money raised by the trial didn't completely cover the cost and the shortfall was made up by donations received after I spoke at a paediatric dermatology conference in Santa

Fig. 115. Mafaldo Soto Valdes making sunscreens.

Fe. The albino booklets were produced by the publishers of my books and paid for by The Royal Society of Medicine in London after I gave a talk there.

The Flying Doctor service, run by AMREF[102] in Nairobi, provided specialist help to small mission hospitals in remote parts of East Africa (not emergency patient care like the Australian Flying Doctor service). As far as dermatology was concerned, the doctors in these remote hospitals would collect up all their patients with undiagnosed skin conditions, or patients for whom treatment was a problem, and get them to come when the dermatologist was visiting for 2 or 3 days. I loved going on Flying Doctor trips. I particularly liked flying in small planes (Fig. 116). Normally we would fly at 5000 feet,

---

[102] AMREF is the African Medical and Research Foundation. It was set up in 1957 by three surgeons to provide mobile health care to remote rural areas in East Africa.

Fig. 116. The author going off on the Flying Doctor service.

which gave a pretty good view of the countryside you were flying over. One of the pilots was very keen on wildlife and would often fly at only 500 feet over the game parks so that we could see the animals. When we got to the destination, the plane would fly around the hospital in circles to let them know that we had arrived. They would then send a car to meet us at the landing strip - a flat piece of grass, sometimes very small. Sometimes we had to fly in circles around the landing strip too, to chase away animals that were grazing there, or children who were playing there. People always knew when the plane was due and usually there was a welcoming committee to greet you when you arrived (Fig. 117).

The work at the destination was very variable. At Ifakara, eight hours flying time from Moshi, I saw only thirty patients in three days, but I spent every afternoon teaching seventy-six students at the Medical Assistant Training School there. On my first visit to Wete, on the island of Pemba, I saw four hundred and sixty patients in two days! The second time I went there, a message was given out on the radio that a dermatologist was coming and that anyone with a skin problem should go to the

Fig. 117. Flying Doctor service: being welcomed when the plane touched down.

hospital. Six hundred patients turned up! A Russian pharmacist ran the skin clinic there usually and she was very helpful to me on each of my visits. She not only translated for me, but also made the ointments that the patients needed on the spot. Every time I visited it was very hot with 100% humidity. Seeing patients was a real pleasure because it meant that I was too busy to take more than a cursory note that my clothes were wringing wet and the sweat was pouring off my face.

Each time I stayed there the hospital put me up in a local guesthouse. It was fine when there was electricity as I had a fan over the bed, which made the temperature in the room bearable. One night the electricity went off at 6.30 pm. I decided to have a shower and go to bed early. I had a shower by the light of an oil lamp, and then, carrying the oil lamp back into the bedroom, I slipped and fell over. At the same time the oil lamp went out leaving me in complete darkness. I managed to find my head torch by feeling my way round the room, and then discovered that oil had leaked out of the lamp all over the floor. I managed to clean it up with some toilet paper. By then I was pretty cheesed off. It was too hot and the batteries in my head torch were low, so I couldn't read. I decided to go to bed. I managed to get off to sleep only to be woken just after 9 pm by a bright light coming on over my bed; the electricity had come back on. I got up and put the light out. I next woke up at 4 am because I was too cold! So I got up again and turned the fan off. Then I was too hot! I managed to get back to sleep and when I woke up at 7 am I was covered in flea bites. Count it pure joy whenever you face trials of many kinds![103] Oh Yes! Interestingly I had taken Corrie ten Boom's book, "The Hiding Place" away with me to read if I had any spare time! I remembered from reading it before that in the concentration camps they were overridden with fleas and were grateful to God for them. It meant that Corrie could be with her sister Betsie and the guards never came into their hut so they were free to worship God every night. I wondered what good was going to come out of me being bitten alive!

On one occasion I was in Pemba for two weeks, carrying out a research project on fungal infections. Because of the high humidity, fungal infections were much more common and much more extensive than they were in Moshi. It meant that I was able to attend the local Christian church on the two Sundays I was there. The island of Pemba is 99.99% Muslim but there is a small Christian community worshipping there. The second Saturday I was there I thought that God said to me, "What you have done so far is not why I brought you to Pemba. I will give you a message for the people here." It didn't seem likely that I would have a chance to say anything, but I decided that if the pastor asked me for a message in church I would know that it was from God and I should speak. The next morning at the end of the service the pastor told the congregation that I had been there for two weeks and would be leaving on the following Tuesday. Then he said to

---

[103] James 1:2-3 (NIV).

me, "And if you have a message to give us we would like to hear it!" So I went to the front and spoke. One of the ladies translated for me. I told them that although they were few and were just a small island in a sea of Islam, it was to **them** that God had given the secrets of the Kingdom of Heaven. I talked about Fatima at Lang'ata[104] and how God can do the impossible if we will only make ourselves available to Him.

At the end an old man stood up and thanked me and said that he would like to give me a gift in return. They also had a miracle to share. He said that there had always been a church in Wete. It used to be a big church on the site of the current police station. In 1976 the Prime Minister of Zanzibar said that they needed the site for the police station, and that they would give the church another site. But they didn't keep their side of the bargain. So in the end the Christians built a church at the site of the old graveyard and it was opened in 1988. He said, "See the church is standing, but the man who was the Prime Minister is not!"

---

[104] See Chapter 11.

CHAPTER 16
OPPOSITION

"Consider it pure joy, my brothers, whenever you face trials of many kinds, because you know that the testing of your faith develops perseverance. Perseverance must finish its work so that you may be mature and complete, not lacking anything"
James 1:2-4 NIV

I have some exclamation marks in my Bible by the side of these two verses from the first chapter of James. Probably that is because I don't like it when things go wrong. In Tanzania I'm not sure that I ever got to the point of considering it pure joy when different kinds of trials came. It is true that some good came out of them (some of them), and we learnt to persevere with what we believed God was calling us to do, but it wasn't easy.

The first difficulty was with a work colleague from Ethiopia. He arrived a month after me, and for some reason didn't like me from the beginning. He wouldn't speak to me even when I spoke to him. It made doing clinics or ward rounds together very difficult. I wrote in my diary after only three weeks of it, "It's going to be hard working with him like this for any prolonged period of time. Maybe I will learn to be more tolerant – I don't know – it doesn't seem possible at the moment (certainly not humanly speaking)." A few days later I was struck by reading, *"Pray for those who persecute you"* in Matthew's Gospel.[105] I determined that instead of moaning

---

[105] Matthew 5:44 (NIV).

about him, I would pray for him. At least I determined to try, and asked God to give me grace to try. In the two years he was at the RDTC he didn't change, and I was never able to count it pure joy that he was like that.

I absolutely loved my work, but there were often difficulties to be got through. When visiting dermatologists came from America and Europe for six months or a year at a time, we had enough staff to do the work, but without them we really struggled. Henning spent most of his time on administration, overseeing the building of the student hostel and then the dermatology building, and all the administrative jobs that go with running a dermatology school. That left only two of us to do the work, and there was a lot of it to do. At one point one of the Swiss volunteers complained at the weekly staff meeting that I was the only person who turned up to do the clinics on time. The others went crazy and thought that I had been complaining. It was all very unpleasant. Some days I wrote in my diary, "I'm not sure how much more of this I can take."

At one time I was on call day and night for 4 months, as well as looking after the ward and outpatient clinics when both of my colleagues were away. At the end of it I was exhausted and developed one infection after another. At one stage my right leg was very swollen and I had to stick a scalpel blade into an abscess on my calf to let the pus out. In retrospect I probably had MRSA, although I didn't realise it at the time.

Later we got some junior colleagues to help, but my western work ethic was a problem for them. And of course misunder-standings arose leading to anger and frustration. We had a microscope stolen from the doctor's office. The door to the office was locked, but two of the louvre windows had been removed and there were fingerprints on the surrounding windows and muddy footprints on the windowsill and the desk next to it. It was obvious where the thieves had got in. I reported the theft to the hospital authorities and through them to the police. When the police came to investigate they said that because the door was locked and had not been forced, the thief must be someone who used the office! I pointed out the fingerprints, the muddy footprints and the missing windows, but they took no notice. They insisted on searching the houses of the two junior members of staff who used the office. I was forced to go with them, and they tore my two colleagues houses to pieces and left them in a terrible mess. Needless to say they found nothing. But there was a lot of resentment that it had happened, and the blame was put on me.

For the first year we were in Tanzania both Jim and I were fit and well in spite of our "bread and jam" diet. But after that we were frequently sick and often didn't know what to do about it. If you feel unwell and have a bit of a fever in the UK, unless there are specific other features, you just assume that it is a viral illness and it will get better. In Tanzania we never knew whether to assume the same, or whether we should do something about it. For example, I woke up one morning with a thick head but otherwise felt OK. I went to the hospital to do my outpatient clinic, but when I got there, I began to sweat profusely and my head began to swim. I decided that I had better get a blood smear taken to check that I hadn't got malaria. It was negative, so I carried on with the clinic. After the clinic I bumped into one of the Tanzanian physicians and asked for his advice. He said I should assume it was malaria, even with a negative smear, and take some treatment for it. But that went against all my principles of how to practice medicine. I was taking regular malaria prophylaxis, we had mosquito netting on all our doors and windows, and we slept under a mosquito net, so I didn't expect to get malaria - and as far as I know I never did.

In 1998 I started getting episodes of tachycardia.[106] For some reason I found them very frightening and every time it happened, I thought I was going to pass out. On one occasion I had almost continuous episodes all night and I was very

---

[106] Rapid heartbeat.

surprised to wake up in the morning and find that I was still alive. Two days later Paul came to visit. It was wonderful to see the joy on his face when he saw that I was OK. He said that he had slept well the night before for the first time in a week. Until then he and his wife had been praying for me day and night for a week. He then read me some verses from Psalm 139, "*O Lord you have examined my heart and know everything about me. You know when I sit or stand. When far away you know my every thought. You chart the path ahead of me and tell me where to stop and rest. Every moment you know where I am. You know what I am going to say even before I say it. You both precede and follow me, and place your hand of blessing on my head. This is too glorious, too wonderful to believe.*"[107]   Even as he read it, I began to cry. "O Lord you have examined my heart." God knew everything about my heart – every heartbeat. Why was I worried?

I ended up flying back to Southampton to see a cardiologist. I had to go alone as Jim was working. I stayed with my stepmother, Grace. She was upset because she didn't know how to help me. I waited 7 weeks before the cardiologist would see me, and then only for 5 minutes! He gave me no advice on what to do, and I returned to Tanzania in the same state that I had been in before I left. While I was in Southampton I read through the Psalms in the Good News Translation. Several stood out for me in a way that they never had before:-

Psalm 6:1-3. Lord, don't be angry and rebuke me! Don't punish me in your anger! Have pity on me because I am worn out. Restore me because I am completely exhausted; my whole being is deeply troubled. How long Lord will this last?

Psalm 6:6. I am worn out with grief; every night my bed is damp from my crying, my pillow soaked with tears.

---

[107] Psalm 139:1-6 (The Living Bible).

<u>Psalm 9:12.</u> God remembers those who suffer; he does not forget their cry, and he punishes those who wrong them.

<u>Psalm 13:1-2.</u> How long will you forget me Lord? Forever? How much longer will you hide yourself from me? How long must I endure pain? How long will sorrow fill my heart day and night?

It was a difficult time. A month after I got back I was booked to speak several times in South Africa at their annual dermatology conference. I umm'd and aahed about whether I should go, as I was still feeling decidedly fragile. The conference organiser arranged for me to see a cardiologist in Cape Town. He was very nice, examined me, and did an ECG and a chest X-ray. He explained all the possible causes and said that I should take a beta-blocker regularly to prevent it happening. He said that if I continued to get episodes of tachycardia while on the pills, then I would need further investigation and he'd be happy to do that. He gave me his card and fax number to get in touch with him if necessary. So that was reassuring. I started the pills, gave my talks, and returned to Tanzania.

I was tired all the time taking the beta-blockers, but I was otherwise well. Six months later I preached at the English service at St. Margaret's Church. After the sermon I thought that God was saying to them:-

1. Some of you have seen God's kingdom, are even in God's kingdom, but you don't want the Holy Spirit to blow where He wants. You're quite happy serving God in your own way. God is saying, "Let me fill you again today with my Holy Spirit and give me a free rein in your life."
2. Some of you are frustrated that God isn't doing things the way you think He should. Bring that frustration to Him today – honestly – tell him of your frustration and your anger – let Him show you His plans.

3. Some of you need God's peace. You are afraid. You lie awake at night worrying and fretting. God says, "Bring these worries to me; let me carry the burden and let me give you my peace."

4. Some of you need forgiveness. God has brought to mind this morning some things that have never been dealt with.

I asked those for whom what I had said was relevant to come to the altar rail for prayer, but there was no response. I waited. No one moved. So I prayed (aloud) telling God that we were Anglicans and shy of getting up in front of people, but please would He deal with all these things anyway. Half way through my prayer people began to come forward. There were people at the rail and people crying in the pews. Paul led them in a prayer of repentance and commitment if they wanted to be born again, and then we prayed for people individually. I got the students to help Paul and me pray for those who had come forward. There was one man at the end who wanted Paul to pray for him a second time. He said that he ran a bar and had been burgled three times in the previous three months. Paul told him that maybe God was telling him he was in the wrong business! After the service Paul was really excited at what God had done. It was the first time that I had preached since I was ill. It was good to do it again and to realize that God hadn't given up on me.

A year later the arrhythmia returned together with profound lethargy. This time I went to see a cardiologist in Oxford. He didn't find anything specific wrong with me and wasn't able to record an episode. He told me that, because the treatment for arrhythmias isn't very good, I might have to put up with episodes every 3-4 months, and have to put up with being out of action for a few days afterwards as the best option! That wasn't what I had wanted to hear.

I asked God what He was saying to me in all this? The main message I think was "Do you trust me?" He was trying to wean me off being so self-reliant. I thought I had given all that up years before, but it had crept back, little by little so that I had come to be "in control" in most areas of my life again. Then when things didn't go the way I wanted them to I got angry and frustrated. Well, I had NO control over this heart problem and the various doctors hadn't been able to solve it for me, so I had no choice but to trust God with it. Easy to say; not so easy to do!

When I got back to Tanzania, Godwin told me that when Paul received my letter from the UK saying what had happened, he had taken it to the English congregation at St. Margaret's Church, read it out, and asked them to pray for me. He said he wasn't surprised that they didn't find anything wrong with me because he was sure that these arrhythmias were spiritual attacks. He said that I had had a profound effect in Tanzania and that the enemy didn't like it and wanted to put me out of action.

At the end of the year, the Bible study group met together to look back at the year that was ending and to look forward to the one to come. We had a communion meal together and then I asked them to share the things that they were thankful to God for. When it came to Clara's[108] turn, she said that she was so thankful to God for sparing my life! When it came to Paul's turn, he said the same, "I am so thankful to God that He spared your life, Barbara." When it came to my turn, I said, "Well I'm not thankful for the last year. It's been really horrible!" So much for counting trials as pure joy! Some days I wondered if I had learnt anything at all in my time in Tanzania.

Being sick was one of the trials we were all prone to. We were ill in lots of other ways over the years. I had two episodes of anaphylaxis to two of the pills I was taking, and we had frequent gut problems from giardia, amoebiasis and shigella.

---

[108] Clara was Paul's wife.

Of course I wasn't the only one. Quite often we found that everyone in the Bible study group was ill at the same time, with all kinds of different illnesses. Paul too was often sick, as were his wife, children and grandchildren. One of his daughters even died. We assumed that Satan was trying to take us out of action, and learnt to hold each other up in prayer like Aaron and Hur held up Moses' hands when the Israelites were fighting the Amalekites.[109] But we had to keep reminding ourselves to do it because otherwise we forgot.

Goodluck, who was a member of the Bible study group, and a neighbour of Paul's, was a local Pentecostal pastor. He had had a new church built with money from an American missionary society. The American missionary who was working with him had gone back to America on a visit and some money was due to be paid to the builder's merchant. With no one around to pay the money, the builder's merchant had Goodluck put into prison. While he was there his wife and two of his children became sick. It was hard to be joyful under such circumstances.

Vicky and I went to visit him in the prison on the Sunday, six days after he had been arrested. I'm not sure what I expected, but it was certainly different to what I found. When we got there we had to give our names and the name of the person we'd come to visit to one of the guards. We then had to stand around outside with all the other visitors waiting to be called. About a dozen visitors were allowed in at a time, for a variable amount of time depending on the whim of the guards. Eventually we got called to go inside. There we found a large metal grill gate. We were on one side and the prisoners were on the other side. We were allowed to talk through the gate but not to go near it. Everyone was talking (shouting) to his or her relative or friend at the same time. It was quite difficult to hold any kind of conversation. But we found

---

[109] Exodus 17:8-13 (NIV).

Goodluck in very good shape. He looked no different to usual and he was thrilled with all that God was doing in the prison. Apparently on the first night that he was there two men were converted, the day before our visit another twelve, and on the day of our visit he had held a service in the morning. He asked us if we could bring in some Swahili Bibles and some exercise books for the new converts as soon as possible.

Apparently the accuser was meant to pay the prison for the accused's food.[110] But the builder's merchant only went to pay some money when Goodluck had been in prison for seventeen days. Had he meant him to starve until then?

All the time Goodluck was in prison, Paul acted as the go-between. Goodluck's lawyer said that if half the money owed could be paid, Goodluck would be released. I asked Henning if he could give me the money that I had spent in England on equipment for the department, which would cover half of Goodluck's bill. He wrote a cheque and his secretary went to the bank and cashed it. I took the money down to Paul at lunchtime, hoping that by taking it to the lawyer we could get Goodluck out of prison that day. Apparently not! The next day Paul gave me the money back. He said that the prosecuting lawyer was going to put a stay on the American missionary's belongings, and since they were worth more than the debt, that should enable Goodluck to be released – perhaps in three days' time! I couldn't understand why no one thought it important to get a move on. Eventually he was released after three weeks. But even though he had done nothing wrong, he had to report to the police station every week for the next three years until the court case was settled. Interestingly Honorata, one of the Tanzanian ladies in the Bible study group, said that her husband had once been put in prison unjustly for five months, but that many blessings had

---

[110] Obviously that cost would be added to the final bill once the case had been settled.

come out of it. He had run classes in the prison and taught men to read and write, and had shared the gospel with them.

The apostle Paul wrote to his protégé Timothy, "*Anyone who wants to live all out for Christ is in for a lot of trouble; there's no getting around it.*"[111] We found that that was true even for us!

---

[111] 2 Timothy 3:12 (The Message).

CHAPTER 17
LOVE ONE ANOTHER

Jesus said, "A new command I give you: Love one another. As I have loved you, so you must love one another. By this all men will know that you are my disciples, if you love one another."
John 13:34-35 NIV

One of the joys of living in Tanzania was to become a surrogate part of Pastor Mtowe's family. We were welcomed as partners in preaching the gospel; Jim as driver was considered just as important a part of the group as those who preached, led services or prayed for the sick. We were also welcomed to be a part of the Mtowe family, to share in their joys and their sorrows. Very early on Paul asked us to take him to Arusha where Beatrice, one of his daughters, lived. She had just had her fourth child and he was keen to see his 13th grandchild. I was asked to pray for the baby and I prayed that he would grow up to be a man after God's own heart. A week later I learnt that they had named him David![112] There was no one in the family with that name.

Three months later we were invited to go with Paul and Clara to the same daughter's home on Boxing Day. We set off early in the morning and went to the service at the Cathedral in Arusha and then on to Beatrice's house for lunch. We sat down and were given sodas very formally, the drinks being poured out for us by one of the women. Then we had our hands washed by having water poured over them so we were

---

[112] Acts 13:22 (NIV).

ready to eat. We sat at a small table and a bowl containing some meat and a very large carving knife were brought out and given to Paul. He was to carve the jaw of the goat that the family had slaughtered for Christmas. It was the lower jaw with the teeth still present and with a little meat attached to it. Paul hacked off the meat and shared it out between the three of us (Paul, Jim and I). We ate it with our fingers and everyone else stood around watching us. Then we were asked to sit at the formal dining table and Clara and two other ladies joined us for the main course, which was a large bowl of cooked meat (goat) and bananas. Paul told us that this was a typical African meal, and that we should make ourselves at home and enjoy it, which we did. After lunch it was back to sit on a settee, drink some more sodas and have our photographs taken with all of the family. We never found out when the rest of the family ate.

There was nothing to buy for people in Moshi to give as Christmas presents, so we took a basket of cakes and a few mince pies for the family we were visiting. After lunch one of the ladies stood up and formally thanked us for the cakes. Then Paul stood up and spoke in Swahili, and the lady who had just thanked us translated his words into English. He said that we were his very dear friends and thanked the family for welcoming us and us for coming. It made us feel very humble, and very privileged that they would open up their home to us as if we were good friends and completely accepted as part of the family.

The following summer a good friend, Wendy, came to visit us from England for a month. We planned to take her on safari to Ngorongoro Crater and to the Serengeti for a week. Two days after her arrival Paul and Clara killed a chicken and brought it for us as a welcome gift to her.[113] At the Bible study group that evening I asked them to pray for me that

---

[113] To cook a chicken was a special treat for us and a welcome break from rice and beans.

I wouldn't waste my holiday on things that weren't God's best for me. Paul prayed that I would go up a mountain and meet with God, and that when I returned I would be radiant and that everyone would be afraid of me![114] Why don't we pray for one another like that in the UK?

A week later we set off for Ngorongoro Crater and arrived at the campsite in the evening. We put up our tents,[115] cooked a meal and went to bed. The next morning we drove down into the crater and saw lots of animals including a group of

Fig. 118. Our Land Rover in Ngorongoro Crater. Spring eating into the chassis.

lions really close up. When we stopped to eat our sandwiches at lunchtime Jim noticed that there was something wrong with the Land Rover. When he looked more closely he found that the springs had gone up through the chassis (Fig. 118). Disaster! What to do? He drove the Land Rover very slowly out of the crater, up a winding, rocky, 1-in-6 road. At the top he drove it to a garage run by the tour company Abercrombie and Kent. They said they couldn't fix it there and then because there was no electricity, but that if we took it back at 5 pm they could fix it for us. They thought that it would only take an hour.

We drove back to the campsite and unloaded everything out of the Land Rover (Fig. 119). Jim took the car to the garage at 5 pm and I prepared our evening meal so that we could eat as soon as he got back. At 8 pm there was still no

---

[114] Exodus 34:29, 30, 34-35 (NIV).
[115] A friend had lent us a tent for Wendy.

Fig. 119. Our campsite on the rim of Ngorongoro Crater: once the Land Rover went to be mended we had nowhere safe to store our food.

sign of Jim returning. A family who were camping quite near to us invited us to sit by their campfire and have a cup of coffee with them while we waited. Interestingly the mother was a GP in Cambridge and knew a good friend of ours! As we sat there being sociable, the son saw a shadow by our tent. When we looked more carefully we saw that it was a hyena. Having no car to put things in, all our food was out in the open. We shouted and threw stones at the hyena and eventually it slunk away. The driver of the family we were sitting with gave us a big black sack. We put all our belongings into that and took the sack back to their campfire. At 9 pm we were getting a bit anxious about Jim, so I asked their driver if he could take us to the garage to find out what was happening. When we got there, having seen two packs of hyena along the road, they had just finished fixing the Land Rover. The mechanic assured us it was now perfectly OK and that it would be fine to drive on to the Serengeti. They had completely rebuilt the rusty part of the chassis.

When we got back to the campsite, we reheated our dinner on our new friends' campfire and ate it sitting with them. We then moved everything back down to our tent, washed up, put everything back in the land Rover and went to bed. I wrote in my diary that night, "It seems as if God is taking care of us; things could have been a lot worse!"

The next morning, after a lot of discussion, we decided to believe what the mechanic had said and drive on to the Serengeti. The road was very bad – corrugated all the way. When we were nearly at the campsite in the Serengeti I spotted three vehicles, which had stopped by the side of the road. We knew that that usually meant something interesting to see, so we headed off in that direction. By the time we got there the other cars had all gone and there was nothing to see. But as we sat by the side of the road wondering what they had been looking at, a leopard walked down the middle of the road just in front of us, and then obligingly jumped up onto a bare tree branch right by our Land Rover (Fig. 120). It was the first leopard we had seen in our two years in Tanzania, and it put all the hassle of the day before into perspective.

Fig. 120. Our first sighting of a leopard in the Serengeti.

Fig. 121. Our campsite in the Serengeti.

We got to our campsite at 5.30 pm, put up the tents (Fig. 121), collected some firewood, lit a fire and cooked our dinner. Just as the dinner was cooked it absolutely tipped down with rain. I dished up our meal and we took it into the Land Rover to eat it. Even though it was still raining I thought I had better wash up, so headed back out into the rain. The sandwich tins, which had contained our dinner before I cooked it, had disappeared out of the washing up bowl where I had left them, and the saucepan that I had cooked the dinner in had also disappeared. I found the saucepan about twenty yards away, licked clean. The next morning we found the sandwich boxes some distance away with teeth marks right through them. Obviously a hyena had enjoyed the remnants of our meal.

The next day we collected a guide from the tourist centre and had a wonderful day driving round the Serengeti with him. In the morning we saw another leopard sitting in a tree, a lion walking along and a cheetah running through the long grass. It was hard to decide which to watch and photograph first. Later as we were driving along we saw another leopard

Fig. 122. Leopard in a tree.

up a tree, and this time we were able to drive right under the tree to get a good look at it (Fig. 122). In the afternoon we saw a cheetah sitting under a tree and then rolling over with its legs in the air and then washing its paws just like a pet cat. Later we inadvertently got between a lion and some buffalo it was stalking. After dinner that night we were sitting on stools outside our tent when two hyenas walked nonchalantly by about ten feet away from us!

The next morning we were woken up by "something" jumping on our tent. It turned out to be baboons playing a game of jumping and bouncing off the tent. They didn't do any damage, but a year later when Jim was camping in the Serengeti with some friends, he got back to the campsite one evening to find our tent completely demolished by baboons and all the poles bent (Fig. 123). We made a leisurely start that day and over breakfast I read out loud the words from Psalm 104. *"He made the moon to mark the seasons, and the sun knows when to go down. You bring darkness, it becomes night, and all the beasts of the forest prowl. The lions roar for their prey and seek*

Fig. 123. The Serengeti: our tent had been destroyed by baboons jumping on it.

their food from God. The sun rises, and they steal away; they return and lie down in their dens. Then people go out to their work, to their labour until evening. How many are your works, Lord! In wisdom you made them all; the earth is full of your creatures."[116] They seemed fitting somehow.

We had another fantastic day looking at animals and birds. We saw the leopard that we'd seen on the first day again, but this time with three tiny cubs. We watched them at their antics for a couple of hours before going to Seronera Lodge for an ice-cold soda. As we walked through the door of the lodge we were greeted with, "Hello Dr Leppard!" It was a man who I had seen in the skin clinic the previous year. Wendy said, "Are you are famous all over Tanzania?" In the evening I wrote in my diary, "It has been a wonderful, fantastic day. This afternoon I felt like turning somersaults and cartwheels, I was so happy. Now I feel like singing for joy, and Paul's prayer eight days ago that I would meet with God on

---

[116] Psalm 104:19-24 (NIV),

my holiday and come back radiant certainly feels like it was answered today!"

The Land Rover survived the holiday but two months later the chassis broke again and we weren't sure how long it would survive on the Tanzanian roads. Just after that happened Paul told Jim that there was to be a Land Rover auction in a few days time where he might be able to get a second-hand chassis. They went to the auction together and Paul did the actual bidding. They got a 21-year-old Land Rover for 120,000 Tanzanian shillings.[117] Paul was like a little kid and jumped on the roof of the new vehicle and waved his arms about as if he'd done something really clever. He then arranged for it to be transported back to our house (on a tractor and trailer). They had gone to buy a chassis, but what they bought also had an engine, differential, some seats and part of the bodywork. We were able to sell all the bits that we didn't need so in the end the chassis and floor only cost us 50,000 Tanzanian shillings.

Jim took his new chassis down to Chuni, our mechanic in town, on the back of a friend's trailer. Chuni then stripped off all the bodywork, removed the engine, gearbox and drive train and everything else from our Land Rover and reattached them to the new chassis. Apparently the floor of our Land Rover was full of holes, so Chuni hired a pickup truck and collected the bodywork that went with the new chassis from our garden and removed the floor of that and put it into ours. Basically everything was removed from the chassis on our Land Rover and put back onto the new (21-year-old) chassis. When it was finished, Chuni delivered it to our house as good as new. He reckoned that it would last another 20 years![118]

In December that year another friend came out to see us to climb Mount Kilimanjaro. Again, Paul and Clara treated him like an honoured guest. We were invited to his granddaughter's second birthday party, which was an amazing experience.

---

[117] £200.

[118] Actually it has lasted 24 years to date and is still going strong.

At one point all the children started to sing spontaneously, firstly happy birthday and then, "Anita you are shining, Anita you are beautiful" and other similar sentiments. It was particularly special because Anita had been born with something wrong with one of her eyes and had had to have an operation at KCMC. The surgeon was an American and she had been terrified of foreigners ever since. Somehow on that afternoon she was able to stay in the same room as us (usually she ran and hid behind the settee if we were there). A few days later our friend, Adrian, returned to record the children singing. He put the songs onto an audiocassette to give to the family for Christmas.

Christmas in Tanzania was not commercialised at all. The Christmas celebrations began on the Friday or Saturday before Christmas with an international carol evening in one of the gardens on the doctors' compound. It was always warm so it was pleasant to be out of doors to sing and eat together. Each nation group chose a carol to sing together. That year the Brits decided to sing, "See amid the winter snow!" There were a couple of rehearsals, which Adrian went to as he has a good singing voice. Jim and I joined in quietly so as not to spoil things. There was also a lot of communal singing, and a talk about the meaning of Christmas by one of the MAF pilots. Then on Christmas Eve there was "Carols by Candlelight" at St. Margaret's Church, and a family service there on Christmas morning.

Paul and Clara invited the three of us to Christmas lunch with their family. Clara had been afraid that we wouldn't accept and was really pleased when we said we would go. They counted it as a privilege that we would spend the time with them. Adrian too was very pleased. He said he hadn't come all the way to Tanzania to eat chicken on Christmas Day, and really enjoyed an African Christmas treat. The day before we had gone to Chekerani[119] to see Vicky who was doing a nursing placement there. She said that we'd made her Christmas by

---

[119] A village near the big sugar cane plantation that we had been to one Sunday. See Chapter 10.

visiting her. In the evening Adrian and I wrapped up about thirty packets of boiled sweets in shiny wrapping paper. We tied them up with ribbon to give to all the children after our Christmas dinner. We gave Paul and Clara a framed photo of themselves taken earlier in the year. When they held up the photo to show everyone, they all ululated to show their appreciation.

The two main things that we learnt in Tanzania was how good it was to live in a loving community and what a difference it made to be thankful for everything. We had so much to learn from our African brothers and sisters.

The following week Paul guided Jim and Adrian along some mountain roads to the offices of the Kibo Estate, where they signed the visitors' book alongside the signatures of The Queen, Prince Philip and Prince Andrew![120] In the grounds of the estate they were chased by a very large tortoise, which was said to be 300 years old. We would never have known to visit such a place on our own.

Adrian left and went back to England on New Year's Eve. The following morning I wrote in my diary, "In this New Year I want to know more of my heavenly Father's love and I want to love Him and serve Him above everything else. There is no doubt that He needs to become more and I need to become less. I pray that humility will begin to show itself in me, and that as a team, the Bible study group will experience God more and more, and that His presence will flow out from us like streams of living water." Of course none of that could happen without the love of our African brothers and sisters.

When my dad died I couldn't afford to go home for the funeral, as I'd only been back to the UK four months earlier to see him when I heard he was dying. I decided that we would hold a service at home at the same time that the funeral was taking place in Southampton. Grace was happy with that and

---

[120] They had been there in 1979.

mentioned it at his funeral. Paul took the service and we had a house full of friends join us including the members of the Bible study group, some other RDTC students and most of the foreigners that we knew. It felt like an opportunity for a proper "Goodbye" among those who loved us.

For the first three years in Tanzania we had no income, but several people gave us money. When I had worked in Southampton I sometimes used to take the service at Southampton General Hospital on a Sunday morning. Those services were organised by a group of volunteers called Hospital Crusaders; one Christmas they sent us a gift of money. A friend in Southampton organised a sponsored walk in the New Forest and raised £1000. We were amazed at their generosity.

Whenever we were ill people prayed for us, brought us meals, and showed us in practical ways how much they cared. It was just what Christians did for one another.

On one of my trips to Dar-es-Salaam for the students' graduation I read "*Through Gates of Splendour*" by Elizabeth Elliot. It is a book about five Americans who went out to Ecuador to try to reach the Auca Indians for Christ and were killed by them. It is an amazing story of the men's faith. Jim Elliott wrote in his diary, "He makes his ministers a flame of fire. Am I ignitable? God deliver me from the dread asbestos of other things. Saturate me with the oil of the Spirit that I may be a flame." Pete Fleming wrote in his, "I am longing now to reach the Aucas if God gives me the honour of proclaiming his Name among them. I would gladly give my life for that tribe if only to see an assembly of those proud, clever, smart people gathering round a table to honour the Son. Gladly, gladly, gladly! What more could be given to a life?" Ed McCully wrote, "I have one desire now – to live a life of reckless abandon for the Lord, putting all my energy and strength into it. I'm taking the Lord at His word and I'm trusting Him to prove His word. It's kind of like putting all your eggs in one basket, but we've already put our trust in Him for salvation, so why not do it as far as our life is concerned?" We were not courageous like those men but the book really resonated with me about what God can do when his disciples are one in heart and mind. I felt so grateful to be part of God's family in Tanzania. But at the same time it was like reading St Augustine. It made me realise the shallowness of my own walk with God and again set me on a course of longing to know Him better. At the beginning of the book[121] are the lines of a hymn:

> "Give of thy sons to bear the message glorious;
> Give of thy wealth to speed them on their way;
> Pour out thy soul for them in prayer victorious;
> And all thou spendest Jesus will repay."

I wrote in my diary, "Lord Jesus, let me spend my life for you. Teach me to hear you and to obey you and let nothing get in the way of that – whatever the cost. So far, you bringing me here to Tanzania has been a wonderful adventure – full of You and of Your sons and daughters who have helped me along the way – but Lord, I think you've hardly begun. Please let me only march to your drumbeat and not try to make my own plans."

---

[121] Elizabeth Elliot. *Through Gates of Splendour*, 1966, Hodder and Stoughton Ltd.

CHAPTER 18
FULL CIRCLE

Simply put, if you're not willing to take what is
dearest to you, whether plans or people, and kiss
it goodbye, you can't be my disciple."
Luke 14:33 The Message

I woke up on the morning of Sunday the 10th of December 2000 with crushing central chest pain, radiating down my left arm. As a doctor I knew I was having a heart attack. I was taken to the intensive care unit at KCMC but their ECG machine wasn't working and they had no drugs. Jim was dispatched into Moshi to buy the drugs I needed from a pharmacy there. Unknown to me the KCMC hierarchy and Henning spent the day arguing about whether or not I should be airlifted to Nairobi for treatment. I imagine there were international calls involved too as the issue was about who would pay the bill if I went. At 4.30 pm it was decided that I should go and AMREF[122] came to pick me up. In the ambulance on the way to the airport they gave me an injection of morphine and I had some relief from the pain for the first time that day. The hospital in Nairobi was just like a hospital in the UK. I was immediately given an injection of a thrombolytic agent,[123] although ideally it would have been given immediately not nine hours after the pain began. A friend who was an MAF[124] pilot flew us back to Moshi six days later when I was discharged. The bill came to £6500, which I had to pay before I could be discharged,

---

[122] Africa Medical and Research Foundation, of Flying Doctor fame.
[123] A drug used to disperse a blood clot.
[124] Missionary Aviation Fellowship.

although later the International Foundation for Dermatology reimbursed me.

A month later I returned to the UK, and through an old school friend who was working at the Brompton Hospital in London I was able to see a cardiologist there. A month after that I had a coronary angiogram and a stent put through the single blocked coronary artery. The cardiologist in London said that I was now as good as new and could return to Tanzania. The International Foundation for Dermatology thought differently. While I was recuperating in Southampton the chairman sent me an e-mail saying that it was time my work at the RDTC came to an end. No one ever said so, but I think that the real issue was money. I had just cost them £6500. What might the medical bills be in the future if I were to become ill again? I guess it was assumed that I was now more of a liability than an asset. I was devastated.

We returned to Moshi so that I could organise a revision course for the current two groups of students and see them through their exams before we left. When we arrived back in Tanzania, Paul Mtowe and one of his nephews met us as we got off the plane. The nephew[125] took our passports and shepherded us through customs in about 5 minutes. When we got back to the house, it was full of friends and masses and masses of roses. Almost everybody that we knew in Moshi was there to welcome us home.

Just before the heart attack I had been writing a book on African dermatology. It was almost but not quite finished. When I thought I was going to die, it was the thing I most regretted - that after all the work that I had put into it, it would never be published. But fortunately I was able to get it finished while I was recuperating in the UK and the company that had published my previous books agreed to publish it

---

[125] The nephew worked at the airport.

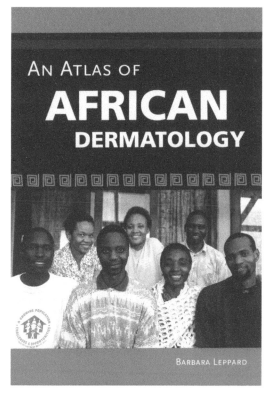

Fig. 124. An Atlas of African Dermatology: a
complete guide to diagnosing and treating
skin diseases in Africa.

even though they knew they would not be able to make any
money from it (Fig. 124).[126]

Our return to Southampton was not quite so joyful. It was
cold. Our house, which we had rented out to pay the bills,
had been totally trashed, and the garden was an overgrown
wilderness. And what was I going to do in the UK? Would I
be able to get a job? Was I fit to work? We were feeling
bereaved. We had lost our jobs, our home, our friends and the

---

[126] It had to be sold in Africa at a price that health care workers there could
afford.

community in which we lived. Most of all we missed our Christian brothers and sisters who knew all our faults but who loved us all the same. It had been such a privilege to live and work with people who were excited about God and yet were so humble and trusting.

Soon after we got home I read in The Message version of the Bible, "*You're blessed when you feel you've lost what is most dear to you. Only then can you be embraced by the One most dear to you.*"[127] I didn't feel blessed. Where was God in our return to the UK? I started thinking about my relationship with God. I decided to draw a picture of it. God was sitting on His throne and I was a small child looking round the door wondering if I dared go in! Earlier in the week I had been reading in Revelation, "*I know your deeds, your hard work and your perseverance ... yet I hold this against you: you have forsaken your first love.*"[128] Those words had pierced my heart like a knife. And I guess it was because of that I wondered whether I dared go in to see God on His throne.

I then found myself reading through the accounts of Jesus' prayer in the garden of Gethsemane. I read all the versions, but it was Matthew's account that I ended up with. "*Then Jesus went with his disciples to a place called Gethsemane, and he said to them, 'Sit here while I go over there and pray.' He took Peter and the two sons of Zebedee along with him, and he began to be sorrowful and troubled. Then he said to them, 'My soul is overwhelmed with sorrow to the point of death. Stay here and keep watch with me.' Going a little further, he fell with his face to the ground and prayed, 'My Father, if it is possible, may this cup be taken from me. Yet not as I will, but as you will.' Then he returned to his disciples and found them sleeping. 'Could you men not keep watch with me for one hour?' he asked Peter. 'Watch and pray so that you will not fall into temptation. The spirit is willing but*

---

[127] Matthew 5:4 (The Message).
[128] Revelation 2:2-4 (NIV).

the body is weak.' He went away a second time and prayed,
'My Father, if it is not possible for this cup to be taken away
unless I drink it, may your will be done.'"[129]

I realised from the story of Gethsemane that Jesus fully
understood how I was feeling. In his greatest agony, he had
taken his three best friends with him and they had fallen asleep
and there was no one to support him. And here we were back
in the UK. It felt like we had lost everything and no one here
understood. I then read, "If you return to the Almighty, you
will be restored,"[130] and "Whoever comes to me, I will never
drive away."[131] We hadn't felt God's presence but that didn't
mean that He wasn't there. And He promised to restore me if
I would turn back to him and regain my first love. I could go
into the throne room – He would not turn me away.

We set about repairing the house. The first week we were
back I spent five days scraping the grease off the kitchen floor.
When I'd finished I realised that if I could physically do that, I
probably could do a day's work as a doctor again. I applied
for jobs and eventually got a job in Southampton. This time
as a Consultant Dermatologist with an honorary university
position, rather than the other way round, which was what I
had before I went to Tanzania.

For the first year back in Southampton everyone at work
treated me as if I was a complete idiot, as if I knew nothing. It
wasn't easy. A friend in America, whose husband was an
ophthalmologist, wrote to me to encourage me. She told me
about Joe Taylor, an ophthalmologist who worked in Africa for
more than thirty years,[132] and who had an outstanding
international reputation.[133] She said that he semi-retired to

---

[129] Matthew 26:36-46 (NIV).

[130] Job 22:23 (NIV).

[131] John 6:37b (NIV).

[132] Some of that time was spent working at KCMC.

[133] Dr Joseph Taylor OBE, FRCS, FRCOphth. See his obituary in
Community Eye Health Journal 1998; 11:1998.

Australia and found that he was treated as if he was a complete idiot; the nurses checked and double-checked everything he did. After a year he'd had enough and went back to being a consultant with WHO and CBM.[134] I realised that I wasn't the first person this had happened to. There is no trial that we go through that hasn't been experienced by others before us. It was helpful to know that somebody understood how I felt. It was only after I'd been back working in Southampton for a year when I gave a lunchtime talk about what I had been doing in Africa, that people began to think that maybe I was OK.

The work at the hospital was no different from what it had been like before I went away except that we no longer had a ward of our own. If a patient needed to be admitted to hospital we had to borrow a bed on a medical ward, which was not ideal. In the clinics patients would often ask for prayer as they had done before I went away. Frequently my registrars would come into my clinic room saying things like, "Mrs so and so wonders if you would mind coming to pray for her." They always stayed in the room while I prayed and afterwards they might also ask me for advice on how to treat the patient medically.

One of the things consultants are asked to do is to visit patients at home if they are unable to get to the hospital.[135] One afternoon I went to visit a patient in a Rest Home only to find that the home was being run by a lady I had seen as a patient twenty-three years earlier. Then she had been a 27-year-old nurse at the hospital and I had diagnosed a malignant melanoma on her left leg. It was cut out and all was well for a while. Four years later she returned with a large lump in her left groin, which turned out to be due to a recurrence of the melanoma in the lymph nodes. These were removed by one of the surgeons. The operation notes said that there were very large glands going

---

[134] Christoffel Blindenmission.
[135] These are called domiciliary visits.

above the inguinal ligament.[136] The pathology showed that the glands were filled with malignant melanoma.

After the operation the wound broke down and she had an open sore in her groin, which had to be dressed daily by the district nurse. The surgeon had been rather blunt with her and told her that the melanoma had come back and that she would probably only have a few months to live. I saw her a month after her surgery as I was then doing a clinic following up all patients who had had melanomas removed. She still had a painful open wound in her groin. It was just before Christmas. She told me that she couldn't talk to her husband about how she felt. He was terrified and couldn't talk to her about it. And neither of them wanted to spoil Christmas for their 5-year-old son. I asked her if she believed in God? "No." I talked to her about Him. I told her some of the gospel stories of Jesus healing the sick. I told her that God understood how she felt and I suggested that she think about telling Him about it and asking Him for help. I spoke to her and her husband separately and then together. A year later she told me that having left the clinic that morning she had talked to her husband and they had agreed together that they would go down to the local church and ask for prayer. When the vicar put his hands on her head and prayed for her, she said that she felt a warm feeling down her back and that she felt completely clean. At that time she hadn't been a Christian and had never read the Bible. She started going to a Bible class with her 5 year old son where it didn't matter that she didn't know anything. She and her son learnt about God together.

On the day of the domiciliary visit, she greeted me like a long lost friend. She was about to be fifty and she invited me to her birthday party. She told me that she now had three sons and that her oldest son was a medical student at St George's Hospital in London (my own alma mater). I have kept in

---

[136] Lymph nodes not only in the groin but going into the abdomen.

touch with her since then. She is now 65-years-old and has never had any further recurrence of her malignant melanoma. I felt like God was really encouraging me on that day when I went to visit one of her residents. Maybe I was supposed to be back in Southampton after all!

At the beginning church was no better than work. I had been used to preaching every other week in Tanzania. I wasn't allowed to do that in England. I was used to praying for the sick. I wasn't allowed to do that in the church as they had their own team for doing that. I was used to teaching others how to pray for the sick. That certainly wasn't allowed. I was used to running a Bible study group. I wasn't allowed to do that.

For the first year after we got back Graham, the vicar, was off sick. Once he was back at work I went to see him to ask if I could train as a Reader.[137] I thought that was the only way that they were likely to allow me to preach. The answer was "No." He didn't know me. How could he recommend me? Our previous vicar, who had known us for more than 20 years, spoke to the new vicar and told him that I was a good preacher and that he trusted me to teach in small groups etc. I didn't know that they had spoken and was surprised one Sunday evening when Graham asked me if I'd like to preach at one of the evening services. I jumped at the chance, and after that I was allowed to undergo the three-year Reader training.

In the final year of the Reader course I had to spend three months in a church as different as possible from my home church. I chose to go to Holy Trinity Church in Weston on a big housing estate on the east side of Southampton. It was in one of the 10% most deprived areas in the UK, well known for having poor academic achievement, high levels of unemployment, and large numbers of single parent families, teenage pregnancies, and high rates of crime and drug use.

---

[137] Readers are now called Licensed Lay Ministers. They are licensed to preach and teach in the Church of England.

My home church was the University Parish Church, full of students and university lecturers. So very different!

I loved it at Weston. It was a small church with a congregation of about 90 and it was very like a family where everyone knew each other and everyone was accepted for who they were, not for what they could do. Having said that, almost everyone in the congregation was involved in some way in the life of the church or in the community. For example one lady befriended an alcoholic man who spent his days walking the streets. Together with four friends she cleaned and redecorated his flat to give him a fresh start. About a year later he was admitted to hospital but discharged himself before he was fully fit. The following Sunday a different lady stood up in church at the time of giving out notices and said, "All of you know Keith. He's been in hospital but he's discharged himself. He still has a catheter in so if you see him, make him go to the doctors so it can be removed!" There was no pretending and no need to pretend.

The congregation was mainly made up of new Christians or those still looking for a faith. There was not much spiritual maturity but they shared their joys and sorrows quite openly, ate meals together, offered practical help to one another and prayed for one another. One lady had her 90th birthday while I was there. The church celebrated it by having a "bring and share" lunch party for her after the morning service to which the whole congregation came. The children, the music group and the vicar provided the entertainment after the meal (Fig. 125).

It was the most welcoming and accepting church that I had ever been to in the UK. It was the nearest I was going to get to being in Africa while living in England. But there was no culture of commitment on the estate, so people turned up to Bible study groups or church services if they felt like it or if they had nothing better to do. One lady came to a small group meeting saying it was either that or sit in her flat on her own. She thought that the meeting was the better of the two choices, but if she didn't like it

Fig. 125. Holy Trinity Church, Weston: Gladys' 90th birthday party and the vicar doing his party trick.

she would leave and go back to her flat! In the main Sunday service there was a mass exodus at the time of the sermon as people took the chance to go outside to have a cigarette.

There was a big emphasis on engaging with the young people in the community, and the church employed a full time youth worker. He had been there for fifteen years when I arrived and was doing a fantastic job. More than half the children on the estate attended the after-school clubs that he ran. When asked at school what was the best thing about living in Weston, most primary school children said it was going to "Rock Solid."[138] Once a month the youth project ran the main Sunday service. Puppets, drama, games, quizzes and sweets are what I remember most. It was a chance for all the children going to the youth club in the week to bring their

---

[138] Rock Solid was the youth group for children aged 7-11.

parents to church on a Sunday.[139] It was an eye-opener for me to see how it was possible to introduce children to the gospel in ways that were relevant and hugely enjoyable.

The ethos of the youth groups (and of the church as a whole) was:-

BELONG ----------------- BELIEVE ------------------ BEHAVE

Belonging comes first. That is the easy bit. Those who belong may later come to believe, and those who believe may later change their behaviour. Lots of kids belonged within the youth project. Some came to believe in Jesus, but changing behaviour seemed an almost impossible dream. Although Jesus says that those who love him will obey his commandments (John 14:15), the youngsters apparently saw nothing wrong in sex before marriage, getting drunk or telling lies. It was a slow old process!

The vicar's vision for the Sunday services was that it would include the 3 Fs:-

- Family. It would be suitable for all the family from the youngest to the oldest. In fact the age of the congregation ranged from infants to 90.
- Fire. It would be full of God and based on Scripture.
- Fun. It would be interactive, multi-sensory and enjoyable for everyone.

It was completely different to what I was used to. I was used to asking people questions when I was preaching or leading services but not getting people out to the front to do things together. How could I engage with young children? Never having had children, my only contact with children over the years had been seeing them as patients, which was not a lot of help. To begin with I had to ask the vicar and his wife for ideas

---

[139] 99% of children attending the youth clubs came from completely un-churched backgrounds.

every week. Later I went off and learnt how to do magic tricks as a way of introducing the gospel to children. That worked very well, particularly in getting the children involved. Everyone was very patient with me and gradually I stopped dreading having to lead "All-Age Worship." There was no expectation that what was done had to be perfect. If someone did his or her best it was received as if it couldn't have been done better.

While I was on my placement in Weston I re-read C. S. Lewis's book, "*The Lion, the Witch and the Wardrobe.*" At the beginning of the story, it was always winter in Narnia but never Christmas.[140] Later, when Aslan came on the scene, signs of spring began to appear.[141] For most of the time since I returned from Tanzania in October 2001, it had felt like winter (spiritually). My placement in Weston was like spring erupting for me. I had been welcomed and accepted for who I was, and it felt like life could now begin all over again. Jim and I decided to change churches and go to Weston permanently. Neither my home church nor the Diocese objected, so at the end of the three months that I was supposed to be there, I just kept on going. Eight months later we moved house and bought a flat in Weston so that we could be part of the community not just the church.

Three days after moving into the parish I was walking along Weston shore with a friend who had come to see our new flat. We could see in the distance a tree with a thick rope hanging down from a good solid branch. As we got nearer we saw a man tying a noose onto the end of the rope. That stopped us in our tracks. Was what was happening what it looked like? I had to find out.

I went up to the man and said, "Are you doing what it looks like you're doing?"

He said, "I might be."

---

[140] C. S. Lewis. *The Lion, the Witch and the Wardrobe*, 1981, Trowbridge: Bookclub Associates, pp. 23, 44.
[141] C. S. Lewis. *The Lion, the Witch and the Wardrobe*, 1981, Trowbridge: Bookclub Associates, p. 77.

We got talking and he said that his life wasn't worth living. He was an alcoholic and no matter how hard he tried, he hadn't been able to stop drinking. He had decided that day that he'd had enough. He would put an end to his life.

I asked him if he was serious about wanting to stop drinking. He said he was. I told him that if he really was serious about it, we could pray for him and that Jesus would take away all desire for drink. "Would he like us to pray?"

"Yes."

So there and then, I laid my hands on his head and asked Jesus to take away all desire for alcohol. I got my friend to phone Jim to warn him that we were bringing someone home for tea and to put the kettle on! I took him home and gave him some tea. After tea I took him home. When I got back Jim said to me, "I suppose this is one of the reasons why God has brought us to Weston!"

I spoke to the man a week later and he told me that he had not drunk any alcohol at all. I spoke to him again 4 years later and he told me he had not touched a drop of alcohol since that day on the beach.

Once we'd moved to Weston it really was like life had started again after 7 years in the wilderness back in the UK. The church recognised the gifts that I had and were happy for me to use them. I was able to preach and lead services regularly, lead a small group, run training courses on how to pray for the sick, and pray in the local doctors' surgery one afternoon a week. I also visited the sick at home and in hospital, took Holy Communion at home to those who couldn't get out to come to church, and prayed for anyone who asked.

It was different to Tanzania. We didn't see demons shouting out in the services whenever we mentioned the name of Jesus, but there was still a lot of demonic activity on the estate. For example, two young women turned up at the church one afternoon saying that all kinds of weird things were happening in their flat. During the night doors were banging, drawers were opening and closing, and things were being thrown at them even though no one else was in the flat. They said they were so scared that they didn't want to be in the flat and they certainly didn't want to sleep there. Two of us went back to the flat with them and commanded the evil forces at work there to leave in the name of Jesus. We then proclaimed God's protection over the flat and the girls who lived there. Immediately the girls stopped being frightened and have had no problems since.

One Sunday when I was preaching I told a story of a man who had sexually abused his daughters when they were young. He was now an old man and losing his memory. When he was prayed for he repented of what he had done to his daughters and received God's forgiveness. Three ladies walked out at that point and another shouted out, "He can't be forgiven for that." The point I had been trying to make was that whatever we had done in the past, we could be forgiven because of what Jesus had done on the cross. What I didn't know, at that stage, was that there were a lot of women in the church who had been abused as children. There were so many women in Weston who had been sexually and/or physically abused as children. I thought I'd heard everything in my life as a doctor, but in Weston I heard things that were beyond imagining. There was pain everywhere.

One of the ladies who came to one of the "Learning to pray for the sick" courses had suffered from eating disorders[142] and all kinds of fears for years. She had no idea of the cause of these problems. She was a lovely Christian lady who regularly read her Bible, prayed and attended church. But she always felt restless and often had migraines. She responded to a word of knowledge[143] when I was looking for someone for the group to practice on. She came forward for prayer a little

---

[142] Anorexia and bulimia.

[143] A word of knowledge is one of the spiritual gifts that Paul talks about in 1 Corinthians 12:7-10. It is God sharing his knowledge about a person with you so that you can know who to pray for or what to pray about.

hesitantly not knowing what might happen, especially since everyone else would be watching. That was the start of an amazing adventure with God, which continued for about 18 months before she came out the other side completely healed. We prayed together on many occasions. Each time we prayed the Holy Spirit revealed something new. It was like peeling the layers of an onion off one by one until everything was dealt with. Each session of prayer took us deeper into this lady's past showing her things that she had been totally unaware of: the horrendous abuse of all kinds that she had experienced as a child at the hands of both her parents, almost from the time of her birth. With each prayer a small segment of those dark memories would surface, together with the pain and fear she had felt at the time. And each time, the turmoil and fear inside her was replaced with the knowledge of the presence of Jesus himself, so that she was able to forgive her parents. She came to realise that she wasn't some "thing" to be abused at will, but a precious child of God, welcomed, loved and accepted by her heavenly Father. He would always love her and she could come to Him at any time. Finally after 18 months she could no longer see the hurting hands of her parents but only the loving, safe and accepting hands of Jesus. Her restlessness and migraines were gone. She had been set free.

This is what Jesus can do, and over the years it was wonderful to see this lady and many others completely healed and transformed by the love of God.

The apostle John ends his Gospel with the words, "*Jesus did many other things as well. If every one of them were written down, I suppose that even the whole world would not have room for the books that would be written.*"

That is just as true today as when those words were written. Jesus is still doing all the things He did when He was on earth. If you multiply my words by the number of Christians living today, there really wouldn't be enough books in the world to reveal all that Jesus has done and is doing.